PRACTICING
JOURNALISM

PRACTICING
JOURNALISM

THE POWER AND PURPOSE OF THE FOURTH ESTATE

Second edition

PAUL STEINLE AND SARA BROWN, Ph.D.

MARION STREET PRESS
Portland, Oregon

Published by Marion Street Press
4207 SE Woodstock Blvd # 168
Portland, OR 97206-6267
USA

ISBN 978-1-936863-63-1

Photos: Paul Steinle (unless noted otherwise)

Library of Congress Control Number: 2012941392

Note: The interviews that form the body of this text were conducted while compiling the reports documented on www.WhoNeedsNewspapers.org. The epiphanies were recorded in a period from June 15, 2010, to July 15, 2011, by the authors, during a reporting trip that included visits to 50 newspapers in 50 U.S. states.

To our colleagues who supported and inspired us in this enterprise:
Paula Barker Duffy, Dennis Beyer, Bruce Garrison,
Sig Splichal and Georgiana Vines.

Contents

Section III: Serving Community

Section VII: Authors' Epiphanies

PHOTOGRAPHS

HD VIDEO

The epiphanies in this book may be viewed in full, high-definition video in the J-Epiphanies section at www.WhoNeedsNewspapers.org.

The texts of these selected epiphanies have been condensed and edited for publication.

Preface

Why We Report:
The Power and Purpose of Journalism

Origins

In 1989, the American Newspaper Publishers Association held its annual conference in Chicago. I stepped into in an elevator and greeted Arthur "Punch" Sulzberger, the publisher of The New York Times. Somehow our conversation drifted into The Times' conversion from black and white to color photography.

Sulzberger appeared deeply concerned about this change. The Times was a conservative newspaper (no comics), and this conversion was a "big deal" for it. I told Sulzberger, "Don't worry." During my broadcast news career, I lived through the conversion of television news from black and white photography to color, and the pictures in color had greater depth and more impact and therefore provided more value to the viewers.

At that time I was just learning about the intensity of journalism values that drove owners and management at newspaper companies, and clearly Sulzberger was deeply involved in his newspaper — he identified with The Times. He had a personal stake in what it was, how it operated, and how it was perceived. And this commitment guided everything he wanted The Times to stand for.

In 1991, when I was about to begin a career teaching journalism at the University of Miami, I first heard the notion that newspapers were in mortal danger. In a discussion with one of the advertising professors, he said, forget about preparing kids for newspapers, they're not going to be around much longer anyway. Since then the predictions of the impending death of newspapers has become a constant refrain.

Eighteen years later, in 2009, my colleagues and I at Southern Oregon University were discussing possible topics for our annual First Amendment Forum. I brought up that widely held perception newspapers were dying and suggested a presentation about the unique contribution newspaper reporting makes to support a community's civic life. The goal was to inform our students what would be lost if newspapers — the main source of local news reporting — disappeared. We selected that topic and devised an ironic title for the event: "Who Needs Newspapers (WNN)?"

Later in 2009, my wife, Sara Brown, and I were discussing what we might do after I retired as associate provost at Southern Oregon University. I had 29 years experience in broadcast news and wire services and 19 years teaching journalism; Sara had worked with newspapers for over 25 years.

We had considered a trailer or camping trip around the USA. Then it occurred to us: it might be fun to devise a mission to make the trip more meaningful. We decided to visit one newspaper in each state in the United States, look behind those stereotypical headlines — predicting newspaper annihilation — and find out, first hand, how these news organizations were actually doing in the digital age.

Valid Sources
In the winter of 2010, to ensure this would be a professional enterprise, we formed a 501(c)(3) nonprofit called Valid Sources. Its broader mission was to discover and share information about how reliable community information (local news) is gathered, confirmed and shared with the public. To address this goal, our first project would examine newspapers' contribution to their communities, and we would post our findings on a website: www.WhoNeedsNewspapers.org.

We recruited colleagues from newspapers, publishing and academia for the Valid Sources board of directors. Then we assembled a group of newspaper industry veterans and experts to advise us in shaping our newspaper project. We called that advisory group our associate consulting editors — our ACEs.

Preparation
To prepare, we conducted a pilot visit to one newspaper. We developed a list of questions, purchased an HD video camera and some lights, and scheduled a visit to The Mail Tribune in Medford, Ore., a town about 10 miles from Southern Oregon University, in Ashland, Ore.

The publisher and two editors from The Mail Tribune agreed to be guinea pigs, and we recorded a dry run with them. After we ironed out some problems, we were ready to go. Our plan was to buy a trailer and truck for our journey to the 48 continental states, and then fly to Alaska and Hawaii.

After several weeks of Craig's List monitoring and some Internet research, we bought a used Chevrolet Silverado four-door, crew cab, long-bed pickup truck and a Keystone Cougar 5th wheel trailer. The truck had a Duramax diesel engine, and the trailer was 31 feet long with one living room slideout.

Selection

A major issue was how to select which newspapers to visit. To get a good mix, we consulted with each state's newspaper publishers association. Initially, we came up with a simple criterion for selection — general excellence award-winning newspapers. Most state newspaper associations run an annual competition for general excellence, so we conferred with them to find leading newspapers in each state for our report.

Later, we also decided to consider newspapers described as innovative to see how they were adjusting in the digital age. We also decided to control the mix to achieve an approximately equal proportion of small, medium and large newspapers; newspapers with diverse ownerships — both public and private; and some specialty newspapers — minority papers; and so-called alternative weeklies.

In this way, we aimed to tell the story of how a wide spectrum of newspapers was doing during this period.

Alaska

In April 2010, we took advantage of a previously planned trip and visited The Anchorage Daily News — Alaska's largest daily newspaper. After their management agreed to talk to us, we arrived at The Anchorage Daily News's offices early one morning and conducted our interviews with the publisher, the executive editor and the person in charge of on-line news.

In addition to a list of specific management questions, we also compiled data for a backgrounder: key facts such as personnel tallies, personnel allocation, coverage focus and some parameters of the newspaper's involvement in Internet activities. We collected samples of their best enterprise stories to post online. Then we took photos of the newspaper's office, some of its staff, its key facilities and its building. All these materials ended up on the WNN website.

This reporting regimen was followed at each of the 50 newspapers we visited.

On the Road

Based on historical weather patterns, we sketched out a driving itinerary that would take us to all 48 continental states and enable us to avoid bad driving weather (Success! We only encountered two days of falling snow in 13 months of travel).

On June 15, 2010, the first leg of our truck-and-5th-wheel-trailer expedition began from Oregon to Oklahoma, with our 6-year-old wheaten terrier, Tallula, in the back of our cab. We were headed for a small, biweekly newspaper in Sallisaw, Okla.

Our experience at The Sequoyah County Times was more or less replicated at every newspaper we visited. In Sallisaw, we interviewed the owner-publisher and the associate publisher — Jim Mayo and his son Jeff — and their managing editor, Sally Maxwell.

They were friendly, cooperative, articulate and professional. Subsequently, at most newspapers, we interviewed each paper's publisher, editor and digital news manager (who functioned under a variety of titles during this period).

The Sequoyah County Times was a small, twice-a-week publication, and the editor and publishers spoke knowledgeably about their community and passionately about their mission to serve that community with reliable information.

They also talked frankly about the problems of running their newspaper at a time when display advertising had decreased and the Internet had taken away much of their classified advertising. (Please listen to the interviews on our website, www.WhoNeedsNewspapwers.org, to judge how frank these newspaper people were countrywide.)

Journalism Values

Several weeks later, when we reached Ohio, we got another inspiration. We started asking each person we interviewed one final question:

Please tell us — in the form of an anecdote — about a time in your career when the power and purpose of journalism became clear to you. What happened, and what did you learn?

The anecdotes these questions evoked were spontaneous, sincere and often heartfelt.

In Dayton, Ohio, Kevin Riley, the former editor of The Dayton Daily News (later, editor, The Atlanta Journal-Constitution) remembered an early murder he covered as a new crime beat reporter.

Riley told us he circled the block in a rough neighborhood, wary to knock on doors and find a victim's mother. "I was very intimidated," he said. "I had made a decision to go back and tell my boss no one was home."

But at that moment, a woman emerged from a house and waved him down. It was the victim's mom.

"What it taught me was," said Kevin, his voice catching, "you read a lot of stories and you may write a lot of stories about people being killed. But you should never forget — it's someone's daughter; someone's mom. It's always stayed with me," he said.

In Philadelphia, Wendy Warren, former V.P. and editor at Philly.com (later, editorial manager, digital, NBCWashington.com), told us about Jill Porter, a columnist for the Philadelphia Daily News. Porter had discovered a scam in which an elderly female patient lost her home while she was in the hospital. After the story was published, local laws were changed to protect such vulnerable persons.

"It was a wonderful moment for this woman, who, I know, nobody else would listen to," said Warren. "Nobody but The [Philadelphia] Daily News."

In Montana, Nick Ehli, managing editor, The Bozeman Daily Chronicle, explained what happened when he wrote about a six-man football team that was formed after its tiny community's leaders converted a beet field to a gridiron on the edge of Custer, Mont.

"I went down to [Custer to] watch a game after this story had run," he said. "This elderly woman came up and said, 'You're the man who wrote the story, right?'"

"'I've only seen my husband cry on a couple of occasions in his entire life,' she told him. 'But he cried when he read that story.'"

In Kansas, Dolph Simons Jr., 83, the chairman and editor of The Lawrence Journal-World, Lawrence, Kan., remembered an historic day when the value of newspapers crystallized for him.

"I was out at my grandfather's house on Dec. 7, 1941 — Sunday," he said. "I heard about Pearl Harbor and Dad said, 'We're gonna put out an extra.'"

Simons' father had preceded him as editor of the Lawrence, Kan., newspaper.

There was no scheduled Sunday newspaper, but they published one that Sunday.

"I always wanted to be in the newspaper business," Simons told us. "I just can't imagine any other business that would be more interesting … and you want to leave your community better than when you found it …"

"I'll be dead one of these days pretty quick," said Simons, "but I would like to figure out how in the hell do we come up with a plan to take advantage of the opportunities to keep newspapers alive?"

"I think we have this responsibility," he said, "to try to inform the public."

Who Needs Newspapers

By July 15, 2011, we had camped in 72 RV parks and traveled 31,000 miles, zigzagging across the USA, from Oregon to Grand Forks, N.D., visiting 50 newspapers.

We discovered a challenged, shrinking, but also rapidly evolving newspaper industry, not the dying business that was widely perceived.

We also encountered an impressive cadre of journalists and publishers in the tradition of "Punch" Sulzberger, Kevin Riley, Wendy Warren, Nick Ehli and Dolph Simons Jr., who owned or managed, edited or reported for these enterprises.

The popular presumption was that newspapers faced inevitable demise, accelerated by digital competition. But 1,200 or so daily newspaper organizations, and several thousand weekly newspapers across the United States, were still collecting and reporting community news and seeking methods to breach the transition from print to the multimedia, multichannel news media world.

With that knowledge, it seemed wiser to wait and see how this evolution turned out before writing a final chapter on the community newspaper industry.

Transformational Newspapers

The newspapers we visited were aimed at becoming transformational multimedia news-and-information companies. Before 1995, newspapers had been newsprint-bound, three-dimensional media — text, graphics and photos. Since then, at widely varying rates of development, they had become Internet-leveraged, interactive, multimedia, multiplatform, news-and-information companies with initiatives in both print and the digital worlds.

Leading transformational newspapers were reshaping their industry. They had added video reporting and video advertising (a new revenue source). Many were using the Internet's interactivity to gather richer feedback from their communities, and a few used feedback data to guide their news coverage and to fine-tune their target advertising. More were devising transactional revenue streams. And some were posting local mini websites to assemble special interest and region-specific audiences for niche advertisers.

A growing number of newspapers — particularly those without the potential to aggregate vast, Amazon-sized audiences — were erecting two-tier websites: One free website and a second-tier website, behind an online subscription fee (a paywall), offering their proprietary content. This strategy had reduced the loss of paid circulation revenue at newspapers such as The Arkansas Democrat-Gazette in Little Rock, Ark., a pioneer in charging for digital content.

We encountered bright, energetic, community-service-oriented journalists and ambitious business managers at these leading newspapers. So an integrated future — in which newsprint would exist side by side with digital news media — did not seem as unlikely as current stories about the demise of the newsprint predicted.

(For more information on this topic, we refer you to a summary of our findings titled: "The 10 Percent Dilemma," at www.whoneedsnewspapers.org.)

Practicing Journalism

Practicing Journalism: The Power and Purpose of The Fourth Estate, is a compilation selected from among the videotaped epiphanies we collected and recorded — which may also be viewed in HD video, online, as J-Epiphanies at our WNN website.

These personal statements are testimony to the quality and commitment of women and men who have chosen journalism as a career. Their epiphanies provide vivid evidence about how journalism and professional journalists serve democracy in the USA.

We hope aspiring journalists will read this book and learn what a career in journalism may yield.

We hope the public will read this book, discover the professional values these journalists embrace and appreciate how these values serve our nation.

And we hope the epiphanies in this book will lift the spirits of professional journalists who work with colleagues such as those whose personal anecdotes are documented here.

Paul Steinle and Sara Brown, Ph.D.

Section I

DIGGING DEEP

Digging Deep

Sometimes the popular wisdom — what "everybody knows is true" — is false. Other times, asking the next question can make or shatter a "great story."

A good reporter must learn what questions to ask and must practice the persistence to ask them. Digging deep also takes determination, a sharp eye, a critical mind and a nuanced tongue.

When an editor at The Seattle Post Intelligencer thought a "juicy sex scandal" was just "too good to be true," her colleague, the metro editor, Kathy Best, ordered a second investigation to verify the facts.

When Seth Tupper, editor of The Daily Republic in Mitchell, S.D., was told his city's building codes required sidewalks in every new housing development, he searched for that regulation and learned the truth.

Both of these quests produced surprising results.

Digging deep has been a classic reporting technique from My Lai to Watergate, but each journey is unique, and the paths often lead to unexpected destinations.

In this section, professional journalists share the epiphanies they experienced when they asked the next question.

"It Really Takes Courage to Go Back and Do It Again"

Kathy Best, editor
The Seattle Times
Seattle, Wash.

When I was working at The Seattle Post-Intelligencer, there had been a series of stories that had been done by many papers — including The Wall Street Journal, all the papers in Seattle, most of the papers in the Northwest — about an alleged child sex ring in a little town called Wenatchee, Wash.

The stories were salacious, and they were really well read, and the whole idea behind it was that there was this ring of adults in Wenatchee, [Wash.,] using religion and other things to prey on these young kids. And I was at The Seattle P.I. as the metro editor.

The editorial page editor — a woman named Joann Byrd — kept saying to us: "This doesn't make a lot of sense; there's something not right about this."

We assigned a couple of reporters, including a metro reporter, to go and start asking questions, because the story had died down and lots of people were in jail. So they went back and started asking questions.

They ended up finding out that what happened in Wenatchee didn't add up; the stories weren't true; people were in jail who should not have been in jail — who were innocent.

Because of the reporting, more than 40 people, who had been wrongly imprisoned, were released. Judges looked at the evidence, and it resulted in many, many changes.

But the aha moment for me was the reaction in the newsroom when we decided to go take a fresh look.

My newsroom was one of the newsrooms that had gone over and done all the: "Wow! Sex ring!" stories.

I had a lot of people, even on the metro staff, that said, "You're betraying us, you know. You don't believe in what we did. You're going to make us look stupid."

That was the moment that I realized, first of all, as the metro editor, you can't make your newsroom happy all the time.

But, as a journalist, that was the moment when I realized it's not enough to report the first time; it really takes courage to go back and do it again, especially if what it's going to show is: You didn't do it right the first time.

That was a pretty critical time, and it's a lesson that stayed with me.

You always, always have to keep asking yourself: "Are you sure you got it right? Are you sure?"

HD video: http://www.whoneedsnewspapers.org/np_interviews.php?npld=epiphany &ivld=epiphany078

Kathy Best joined The Seattle Times in February 2007 as managing editor for digital news. In March 2011, she became managing editor in charge of content creation, working on stories with reporters, editors, photographers and videographers throughout the newsroom. In September 2013, she was named editor.

Before joining The Times, Best was the assistant managing editor for Sunday, national and foreign news at The Sun in Baltimore. She was assistant managing editor/metro at The St. Louis Post–Dispatch and at The Seattle Post–Intelligencer.

"You Are Doing a Public Service"

Ken Doctor, author
Newsonomics
Aptos, Calif.

I was 25 when I was editor of an alternative weekly newspaper. We were competing against The Eugene Register Guard, which is one of the better small city dailies in the U.S. If I were a marketer, I never would've competed with them, but we were competing because we thought it was a good thing to do.

I remember there was a county commissioner who had changed his vote — this is like prototypical local politics — on a freeway interchange. We couldn't figure this out, and in environmental politics — this is in Eugene, Ore., in the 1970s — everything was environmental politics. You tried to build anything — somebody would try to stop you.

He turned around on building a freeway and building a freeway interchange in an area where people didn't want a freeway interchange. We did investigative reporting on it and found that a local developer had paid him off to do that.

Our little struggling weekly, which was always on the edge of bankruptcy — actually would have been in bankruptcy, but we didn't have any assets anybody would want — was able to get that story out there and have that story recognized and have that story be picked up by other media, because it was true. Have that county commissioner taken to court and convicted in court, and the developer exposed.

That taught me — at the tender age of 28 or so — what you can do.

That's what American journalism means: That if you do your work and you do it fairly, you are doing public service.

We knew why we were doing it. The public knew why we were doing it. And it sustained us, when we were paying ourselves $300 a month.

HD video: http://www.whoneedsnewspapers.org/np_interviews.php?npld=epiphany &ivld=epiphany061

Ken Doctor, a leading news media industry analyst, is the author of *Newsonomics: Twelve New Trends That Will Shape the News You Get* (St. Martin's Press, 2010). His Newsonomics.com is a daily, updated web companion to the book.

As an industry analyst he covers the transformation of the news media, as it moves from print and broadcast to digital, focusing on changing business models and the journalism created.

His experience includes 21 years with Knight Ridder, as well as time spent in the worlds of magazines, alternative journalism and syndication.

"It's About Time — That Stuff Has Been Going On for 100 Years"

Geri Ferrara, editor
The Dominion Post
Morgantown, W.V.

We did one of our Spotlights on Government stories, and it was on the local health department. I'm sitting at my desk, and we're to the point where the stories are filed, and we're looking at the data and we're down to graphic stuff. So I asked for a copy of the salary things; I wanted to have a chart.

I'm looking at it, and it says here that the director makes — we'll say — $10 and the assistant director makes $20 and then this, that and the other thing. And I was like: "Cassie!" I called the reporter. "We have a problem here. There's something wrong with this chart. It says the assistant is making more than a director. That doesn't make any sense. Call them and see what the story is."

Called them, and guess what — it was accurate. It led to a huge story. It turned out the assistant director was, in fact, making more than was allowed by law.

We were just looking at a nonprofit organization that was going to be building a new community theater. And some time had gone by, and we realized that — I think it was $400,000 in government funds — grant monies were given to that organization through the county commission. They went to build, and they had no money.

Of course it struck us: How could they have no money if they had $400,000?

Well, they misused the money. It wasn't a vicious thing, but they decided to pay "Paul" a salary from that money instead of the money that was earmarked for construction or something along those lines.

When those things happen, it's very satisfying because you have readers who contact you and say: "It's about time — that kind of stuff has been going on for 100 years, and nobody bothers doing anything because it's so-and-so involved."

I take great pride in the fact that I don't care who you are. Every DUI, for instance, runs in this newspaper.

Every newspaper — I'm sure you're going to run into this everywhere — hears about the conspiracy theory. The smaller the town, the bigger the conspiracy theory: It depends on who you are if you get into the newspaper. What's your name — is if you get into the newspaper.

The reality is that in most newspapers that's the farthest thing from the truth.

I wish we knew what people thought we did. I wish.

My God, we'd be as big as The New York Times. But the reality is we don't know everything.

But standing up for that truth, justice and the American way — to steal the phrase — you're reminded of that when you do stories like that. And people are grateful that you did them.

HD video: http://www.whoneedsnewspapers.org/np_interviews.php?npld=epiphany&ivld=epiphany004

Geri Ferrara became editor of The Dominion Post in 2003, bringing with her more than 20 years experience in the community newspaper field.

Ferrara was trained in Gannett's News 2000 community newspaper program. The corporate-wide Gannett initiative trained editorial departments to understand the value of local news coverage, diversity, reader outreach and interaction, and the principles of First Amendment journalism. She later became a program facilitator. Ferrara graduated from "Gannett University," and was promoted to her first post as a weekly newspaper editor.

She eventually oversaw the operation of five Atlantic County (N.J.) weekly newspapers before returning to The Daily Journal, an 18,000-circulation six-day paper, as assistant city editor. During the course of her career, she served The Daily as city editor, editorial page editor, special projects editor and managing editor.

In 2001, Ferrara took early retirement to partner in the acquisition of a weekly newspaper, The Island Journal, in Brigantine Beach, N.J., where she served as vice president, editor and publisher.

"We Came Across a Situation That Just Didn't Look Right"

Miles Forrest, publisher
The Courier
Houma, La.

More than anything else, you see the impact that the newspaper can have in its ability to shine a light where there has not been one before. One story I remember, particularly, was back in the '70s.

We decided to take a look at prescription sales to the jail and who was selling those prescriptions, what they were charging for those prescriptions and how whoever was selling them was able to do it.

I was in the business department at the time, but the reporter and I had a pretty good relationship, and there were a lot of numbers involved, so he came and he'd sit with me every night, and we'd go through numbers and do computations.

I got involved in this story just right on the edge, but enough to be there while it was being developed and to go through the process.

As a result of that story, everything changed — in terms of the story we were writing, the situations we were writing about — but [also] in terms of my appreciation for what we did and how it could impact the community, and certainly in a very positive way.

We weren't out on a crusade, but at the same time we came across a situation that just didn't look right, and it turned out it wasn't right. We were able to affect it and affect it in a positive way in our community.

HD video: http://www.whoneedsnewspapers.org/np_interviews.php?npld=epiphany &ivld=epiphany056

Since 2000, **Miles Forrest** has been the publisher of both The Courier in Houma, La., and The Daily Comet in Thibodaux, La.

Forrest, a Thibodaux native and graduate of Nicholls State University, began his newspaper career in 1973 at The Houma Daily Courier. He has worked for The Courier or The Daily Comet in a variety of positions ever since.

Forrest is a past president of the Louisiana Daily Newspaper Association, the Louisiana Press Association, and the Louisiana Press Association Foundation.

"Chipping Away at the Edges"

**Bob Gorman
(Former) Managing Editor
The Watertown Daily Times
Watertown, N.Y.**

My first big story was in South Carolina. I was working at a twice-a-week newspaper, and I was covering court.

And all of a sudden all these people show up, and they were pleading guilty to food stamp fraud. I looked at everybody and I thought: Well, this is really interesting. What happened here?

What had happened is all these people had created dummy families and were getting food stamps for three families — not just one family. They were creating entire out-of-whole-cloth people. None of these people had the education, background and sophistication to do that.

So, we could have printed a story that 30 people pled guilty yesterday to food stamp fraud, but I just kept looking at it and looking at it.

Turned out there was a huge scandal brewing within the Department of Social Services for lax oversight, and a lot of people just going through the motions in that department. Whatever anybody came in and said — they agreed; they bought it.

Just by chipping away at the edges, all of a sudden, there's a grand jury investigation and it ended up 100 people were involved. Well, I guess journalism mattered that day.

There was a van that crashed in our town. The van was on its way to Myrtle Beach and its axle broke. The van rolled over, and there were 14 people in the van. Somehow — miraculously — nobody was killed. These were all people who had been going up to Myrtle Beach to change sheets.

Myrtle Beach has all these motels and hundreds of people — poor people who can't get a job in their own little community — and they drive 30, 40, 50 miles one way, in vans, change all the sheets and go back home. People were taking vans that were made for seven people, taking out the seats, putting in benches and carrying all these people.

I got the accident report, looked at it, and I checked with Ford Motor Co. Ford said the van is made for seven. I started checking with the state, and they said: "We license, but we don't certify the capacity for people in there." They just overlooked an entire element, and all these vans were overpacked — waiting for somebody to get killed.

We wrote these stories and the state changed the law.

People lost money — the van driver who was charging everybody, packing people in like sardines. But the state's a safer place because of journalism.

I did those stories very early in my career, and if it wasn't for journalism I can say: It's chaos out there without journalism — that's the world.

HD video: http://www.whoneedsnewspapers.org/np_interviews.php?npld=epiphany &ivld=epiphany008

Bob Gorman was the managing editor of The Watertown Daily Times.

A native of Detroit, Mich., he was graduated in 1974 from Randolph-Macon College, in Ashland, Va.

Before moving to Watertown in 1994 to become assistant managing editor for The Times, Gorman was a reporter and editor for 20 years at newspapers in South Carolina, and was named the state's journalist of the year in 1979. He was named managing editor of The Times in 2002.

In 2001 Gorman served as president of the board of directors for the state bureaus of the Associated Press. He is also a member of the Associated Press Managing Editors Association.

Gorman retired from The Daily Times in July 2013 to become the CEO of the United Way of Northern New York.

"I Stumbled, My Freshman Year, into Discovering a Secret Document"

Tom Rosenstiel
(Former) Executive Director
American Press Institute
Washington, D.C.

Many people have the experience of when they first decided that they might want to be involved in journalism. For me that was when I transferred to a high school that was 100 percent black the year before I went.

To desegregate the school, they allowed students from all the communities to take the summer and invent the school from scratch.

What would an ideal school look like if the students and faculty would start over and invent it just the way they want it?

This was 1971.

I was recruited that summer to work for the school newspaper by an upperclassman, Mike McCurry, who was later Bill Clinton's Press Secretary.

They said, "Well, in this ideal school, we're going to let the students run this newspaper entirely, and we'll encourage them and tutor them, but they won't be supervised in the traditional sense. They'll write it the way they want to write it."

The school board was so up in arms over the freedom that we were given that they wanted to fire the woman who was the supervisor of the student newspaper.

We ended up at school board meetings trying to defend our editor or our publisher from being ousted by the school board.

I realized, as a friend of mine put it, that the lessons in this particular school were as much on the playground and at the school board meetings as they were in the classroom.

And I thought: The way to learn this lesson is to work for the school paper.

Then I went to a college that was the first integrated college in the country and founded by abolitionists, and I stumbled, my freshman year, into discovering, along with another student, a secret document from the admissions office that they wanted to now limit black enrollment at the college, which was pretty scandalous for this particular institution.

When we published that, it went right to the foundations of the university, and I thought: Gee, this newspaper stuff is pretty, pretty potent. It gets right to what people are thinking about and why they're here and why they live here.

This is cool. You do this and people talk about who they want to be. Not too many things can do that.

Those are two examples that occurred in my life when I was quite young, before I knew I wanted to be a journalist, but they probably had some effect on my ending up where I did.

HD video: http://www.whoneedsnewspapers.org/np_interviews.php?npId=epiphany &ivId=epiphany088

In September 2013, **Tom Rosenstiel** joined the American Press Institute as executive director. Prior to that, he designed the Project for Excellence in Journalism (PEJ) at the Columbia University Graduate School of Journalism. In 2006, PEJ became affiliated with the Pew Research Center, where Rosenstiel directed its activities.

Rosenstiel was the editor and principal author of PEJ's "Annual Report on the State of the News Media." He also directed the PEJ's other research efforts, including the News Coverage Index and the New Media Index.

In 2010, Rosenstiel, with Bill Kovach, wrote *Blur: How to Know What's True in the Age of Information Overload*. Rosenstiel and Kovach also wrote: *The Elements of Journalism: What Newspeople Should Know and the Public Should Expect* and *Warp Speed: America in The Age of Mixed Media*.

Rosenstiel is vice chairman of the Committee of Concerned Journalists. He previously was a media critic for the Los Angeles Times and chief congressional correspondent for Newsweek.

"The Difference Between Newspapers and Some Guy with a Computer"

Jay Seaton, publisher
The Daily Sentinel
Grand Junction, Colo.

I'm a college football fan. My team's Kansas State University. Kansas State had a coach who they thought was going to be just wonderful. He replaced a legend. And he failed. His name is Ron Prince. He got fired, so Kansas State's in the process of looking for a new coach.

It's during this season, and there's a coach at Texas Christian University named Gary Patterson who's very successful, and he's a K-State grad, and everyone thought Gary Patterson's a likely next coach.

So the newspapers are covering the coaching search, and there's one blogger (gopowercat.com) in particular — one guy — who's been very successful at providing recruiting news, and how people are doing in practice, and all the stuff that football fans love.

We eat that stuff up, except it's all through one guy. He's got some sources in the athletic department, but it's not responsible journalism. It's just one guy.

So the old legend Bill Snyder is talking about coming back. It's a possibility that he would come back and coach. But a lot of people want Gary Patterson — the guy from Texas Christian.

So this blogger, in his successful website, has apparently broken the story. He strips across the top of this website: "It's Patterson!" The new coach is Gary Patterson. He had details about the terms of his contract and all that. Anyway, it's just not true. He got burned by a source. The newspapers didn't go with it.

The newspapers have an editorial process. The local newspaper, which happens to be my family newspaper — The Manhattan Mercury — knew there was something wrong because they weren't just dealing with one person; they were dealing with a group of editors and the editors were asking questions and forcing the reporters to seek additional sources.

So when they really looked into it — when they really vetted it — they realized it wasn't Gary Patterson at all, it was Bill Snyder.

That showed me the difference between newspapers and just some guy with a computer terminal. It demonstrates what newspapers can do to continue to be the most important voice in their community.

HD video: http://www.whoneedsnewspapers.org/np_interviews.php?npId=epiphany &ivId=epiphany085

Prior to **Jay Seaton**'s arrival at The Daily Sentinel in August 2009 as publisher, he was a corporate and commercial litigation partner at the law firm of Lewis, Rice & Fingersh in Kansas City, Missouri. He also worked in toxic tort litigation at the law firm of Shook, Hardy & Bacon.

Since arriving in Grand Junction, Seaton has become involved in the Colorado Forum, the Grand Junction Economic Partnership, the Grand Junction Forum, the Saccomanno Higher Education Foundation and the St. Mary's Hospital Foundation.

Seaton holds a bachelor's degree from the University of Wisconsin, Madison, and received his juris doctorate from Kansas University in 1996.

"We Were Multimedia Before We Knew What It Was"

Wayne Snow, managing editor
The Opelika-Auburn News
Opelika, Ala.

I was bureau chief for UPI in Tallahassee, and there is a lot of pressure in wire service work. We were multimedia in those days before we knew what it was.

You'd write a story for whatever cycle you were on, you would take the same story and write it for broadcast, then you would take the same story and write it for the next cycle.

I would write those stories and go out for lunch, and then you would turn on the radio in your car, and they're reading the copy that you've just written. You can kind of mouth along with them — even the part that says, "Pause here." That was always a chilling moment.

In particular, one story there emphasized that you really, really, really better get it right. It happened to be a story out of Marianna, Fla., of a doctor who had made some claims about a battery plant on the Apalachicola River causing a high incidence of cancer downstream. Then he claimed that he was knifed and cut up by some people who had lured him out to a place to help them with some kind of problem they were having.

Well, come to find out the attack was made up. That this was a medical doctor who had cut himself up to make it look like he had been attacked.

We got that story before AP, and if you're sitting there with a big national A-wire story — you're first, you want to be first — but there's a little part of you that said: It would surely be comforting if somebody was out there ahead of us on that. But you're out there by yourself on something that you know is going to get picked up by every media organization in the country.

It's a lot of pressure, a lot of fun, a lot of adrenaline. And, yeah, it counts — it matters. You better get it right. And we did.

HD video: http://www.whoneedsnewspapers.org/np_interviews.php?npld=epiphany &ivld=epiphany052

Wayne Snow's job as managing editor comes as the icing on a long career in journalism that began in January 1976. He spent 22 years at The Atlanta Journal-Constitution, where he was at various times a page designer, front-page news editor, politics and government reporter and graphics reporter. He also wrote travel pieces and journeyed to Ukraine in April 2006 to cover the 20th anniversary of the nuclear disaster at Chernobyl.

Snow retired from Atlanta in July 2007 and began work in Opelika the following month. Prior to Atlanta, Snow worked at a variety of newspapers in Georgia and North Carolina and was bureau chief for United Press International in Tallahassee, Fla.

"We're Following the Reporters"

Paul Tash, chairman and CEO
The Tampa Bay Times
St. Petersburg, Fla.

I was at lunch with some reporters, and they said a funny thing happened today.

A house caught fire out on one of the island communities, and it turns out it was owned by one of the ministers in town. His wife set fire to it.

It wasn't a parsonage. It wasn't his permanent address. It was a house he owned just a few miles away from the official residence in a part of town where he is basically unknown.

This was the man who was the president of the National Baptist Convention, which described itself as the largest African-American church in America.

It had been set fire by his wife because she discovered that he had a relationship with another woman, who was also an occasional resident of the house.

So we took an interest.

One story led to another, and it became clear that the Rev. Henry Lyons had concocted the story of the National Baptist Convention as being this huge organization, when in fact it was a fraction of the size he was describing. It was a con that had even been featured, unwittingly, on the front page of The New York Times as a story about how this minister had been so sophisticated.

Yet with a match and some kerosene, one day, his wife, sort of, sparked our interest — if you will.

The stakes were very high. It was a very sensitive story. There was initially some criticism of the paper by the minister that it was racially motivated, biased, prejudiced work, so I was very much involved in it.

Each night I would go home and think: Oh, my God, I can't believe that's true. Yes, I know it is because we've checked, and we're sure of the work. But how can that be true?

One thing would just cascade to another, ultimately leading to the arrest, prosecution and conviction of the pastor, and a prison sentence.

I would have readers come up to me saying, "I can't wait to go to my driveway to see what you're going to have today."

At one point a judge in the case asked the prosecutor, "I can't really tell, Bernie, whether you're following the reporters or whether the reporters are following you." And he said, "Oh, there's no doubt. We're following the reporters."

It was one of those moments and one of those stories that you feel fortunate to have had a part of at any time in your career, and a little wistful that you may not get another one like that again.

HD video: http://www.whoneedsnewspapers.org/np_interviews.php?npld=epiphany &ivld=epiphany048

Paul Tash is chairman and CEO of the Times Publishing Co., owner of The Tampa Bay Times (formerly The St. Petersburg Times).

Tash started with The Times in 1978 as a local news reporter. He also has been a Tallahassee reporter, the city editor, metropolitan editor, Washington bureau chief and executive editor for The Times. From 1990–91, he was the editor and publisher of *Florida Trend*, a statewide business magazine owned by the Times Publishing Co.

Tash is chairman of the Poynter Institute for Media Studies, a school for journalists, which owns Times Publishing. He also serves on the boards of the Pulitzer Prizes, the Associated Press and the Newspaper Association of America.

Tash graduated summa cum laude from Indiana University in 1976. He received a Marshall Scholarship and graduated magna cum laude with a Bachelor of Law degree from Edinburgh University in Scotland in 1978.

"You Can Dig and Dig and Dig"

Seth Tupper, editor
The Daily Republic
Mitchell, S.D.

I was city hall reporter here, and I was doing a story, and my editor at the time had come to me and said that his kids had to walk to school in the street. In his neighborhood, there were big segments where there were no sidewalks, and it always bothered him, and he wanted to approach that issue and figure out what's going on.

We did a series of reports on that, and during one particular story I talked with a city official about the city sidewalk code, and he quoted all these sections of the law. So afterward, I looked up the law on the city website where the city code is, and I couldn't find the sidewalk law — the law that requires sidewalks to be built as part of any new development, anywhere in the code.

I called this official back. "Well, it's gotta be there," he said. "It's gotta be there" And I said, "Well, show it to me. I can't find it."

It wasn't there.

I went to several more city officials, and everybody was perplexed. They said, "It's gotta be there. It's gotta be there."

Well, through the process of digging and reporting, I found out that the city's attorney had accidentally — during the adoption of a totally unrelated ordinance — inserted the wrong code reference in it. He accidentally repealed the law that required people to build sidewalks in Mitchell. So we reported that, and at the very next city council meeting, they had to adopt an emergency ordinance to reinstate this law.

Today Mitchell has been praised for having one of the most progressive and aggressive sidewalk programs in the state. We don't deserve all the credit for that, but I think we deserve some of the credit for making that an issue. We have a much more pedestrian- and handicapped-friendly city today because of it. If you walk around the city you'll see lots of fresh sidewalks and lots of new ramps and things for handicap and ADA accessibility.

That drove home for me the importance of: If we're not here, who's going to do this kind of reporting?

As a reporter you have a choice a lot of times with a story you can say, "Well, I'll just file this thing and get done with it." Or, you can dig, and dig, and dig. Persistence is important, and we should never take for granted the impact we can have if we put our minds to it.

HD video: http://www.whoneedsnewspapers.org/np_interviews.php?npld=epiphany &ivld=epiphany099

Seth Tupper was named editor of The Daily Republic in 2010. Before joining the newspaper in 2003, he worked nearly two years as the sports editor at The Worthington (Minn.) Daily Globe.

Tupper earned a bachelor's degree in journalism with a political science minor from South Dakota State University. While at SDSU, he was editor of SDSU's student newspaper, The Collegian.

"Asking [Questions] for Everybody"

Andrew West, managing editor
The Delaware State News
Dover, Del.

I switched over to the news-side and was working in a small community down at the beach for The Daily Whale (Dover, Del.) newspaper. And there were a couple of things there that I really felt needed to be reported on.

A student was really hurt in a school fight — [and some parents came to me and said] "We need some answers. They're not telling us what is happening inside the school." You know, [that's] when you get that sense that: I'm representing the public and I want answers.

We had a mayor who wanted to fire his police chief in that same small community some years ago, and I remember him telling me that it wasn't my business. I said, personally, it may not be my business, but I'm here representing the public.

That's what I want you to understand — I'm asking [questions] for everybody who lives in this community. To see people not give you answers to questions like that, the more it instills in you that we're here for a reason. We're here to hold people accountable.

There was never really one thing in my career that did that. I think we just experience that daily.

HD video: http://www.whoneedsnewspapers.org/np_interviews.php?npId=epiphany
&ivId=epiphany028

Andy West has served as managing editor of The Delaware State News since 1996. He joined The Delaware State News as sports editor in 1990. Before that, West served as editor of The Daily Whale, Sussex Post and Leader & State Register for Independent Newspapers.

West graduated from the University of Delaware in 1985 with a bachelor of arts in English/journalism. In the early years of his journalism career, West worked for Gannett's News Journal in Wilmington, Del.; USA Today; The Saratogian in Saratoga Springs, N.Y.; The Reporter in Lansdale, Pa.; and the family-owned Reading Eagle Co. in Reading, Pa.

"Maybe the Details Were Just a Little Too Good"

Fred Zipp, (former) editor
The Austin American-Statesman
Austin, Texas

Several months after I started as a reporter in Beaumont, Texas, in 1979, a couple things happened. First of all, it started to rain one night. Before the rain stopped, we had something like 10 inches in 10 hours of rain, which, even by the standards of the Gulf Coast, was unusual.

Toward deadline, an oil tanker exploded at a shipping terminal about a mile away from the bureau where I worked. It was pretty clear, immediately, that there were people on board, and that there were casualties.

This was long before the existence of cell phones, so I had to find a pay phone and sit on it, so nobody else could use it, so I could talk to the city desk.

About every 10 or 15 minutes I would call the city desk and parcel out little bits of information and dictate the story to them. Ultimately, several Korean sailors were killed on the boat.

The next night, it had cleared off and it [had been] a beautiful day, and I was wrapping up for the week, and the city desk called me and let me know there was a guy at a bar down the road from the bureau who had called in to say he was on the ship, which, I recall, was the Sea Tiger. He was ready to give me his first-person account of the night's event.

So I went to the bar and interviewed the guy for several hours, and got just great stuff. That was on a Friday night.

I drank a few beers — went home to sleep — probably hadn't gotten much sleep for two days at that point. Woke up Saturday morning to write the story, and it occurred to me that maybe the details were just a little too good on what this guy had told me.

So I went back to the terminal and asked whether it had a sign-in sheet for people who had come in and out of the gate. They said yes. I asked: Is it possible to look at the sheet? And they showed it to me, and the name of the guy, who I had interviewed in the bar the night before, was not on the sheet. So I asked: Is it possible that somebody could've gotten through the guard shack without signing the sheet? And they assured me that was just not possible.

So I called the city desk, and after a little bit of discussion we decided that — good as the eyewitness account from the night before was — probably no sense in coming in to write it, cause, we just didn't know if it was true or not.

That was a huge learning experience for me. We can invest a whole lot of work in stories we think are just great, but we have to have the courage to pull the plug on them if we're not absolutely certain they're accurate. I learned [that] early on, and I've tried to apply it often since then.

HD video: http://www.whoneedsnewspapers.org/np_interviews.php?npld=epiphany&ivld=epiphany058

Fred Zipp spent 32 years in daily newspaper journalism, most recently as editor of the Austin American-Statesman. He began his career in Beaumont, Texas, and then worked in West Palm Beach, Fla.

Zipp graduated from Duke University in 1977 with degrees in history and French.

Zipp retired as editor from the Austin American-Statesman, Sept. 1, 2011, at age 56. Zipp was with Cox newspapers for 26 years. He is currently editor in residency, University of Texas.

Section II

INFLUENCING CHANGE

Influencing Change

An activist, change-agent mentality abides within community journalism. It flows directly from the mission of public service, embolded by a recognition of news media power. Some journalists embrace this activist role. Others are wary of pursuing it. But any close examination of this industry reveals newspapers instigate change.

Reporters instigate change overtly — through watchdog reporting. Editors instigate change subtly — by identifying a community's agenda of concerns and emphasizing those agenda topics in story assignments.

Appeals for change often appear forthrightly in editorials. But change is also initiated by compelling news stories that shed light on unfair or unethical practices and reports that reveal malpractice, troubling facts or unacceptable outcomes. Nonetheless, reporters and editors who produce and assign investigative reports are sometimes surprised by the power they wield.

In this section, professional journalists share personal epiphanies about how journalism's power to affect change became apparent to them.

"The Written Word is Powerful"

Zach Ahrens
(Former) Advertising Director
The Grand Forks Herald
Grand Forks, N.D.

For me, the eye-opener was in Iowa.

Iowa is a big political state, and I was the publisher of two tiny little newspapers, together, combined, a circulation of maybe 4,000 — little weeklies — and presidential hopefuls would stop by and court such little newspapers. It reminded me that the written word is powerful, and we can influence our readers.

Many people would come to this small property to try to get our support on different issues. From a more lighthearted perspective — any time people don't get their newspaper, their world is shot. It reminds you of the credibility of the product we have. It's going to last.

One of the things people had asked me, they said, "Do you really want to move up there to Grand Forks? I hear newspapers are dying." I said, "I wouldn't have invested in a newspaper — I wouldn't have invested in this company — if I thought that was true." It goes back to the fact that we're still growing. We've repurposed ourselves.

Any time another industry repurposes itself, they call it innovative. In the newspaper industry, they think it's survival. In fact, we're making very good money in print and were making very good money online. I think of it as if my stocks have split, and I've got two piles of chips that are going up. It's been very positive, and it's fun to prove people wrong when they see the results.

HD video: http://www.whoneedsnewspapers.org/np_interviews.php?npld=epiphany &ivld=epiphany102

Zach Ahrens has spent much of his career leading and training advertising teams to sell both print and online advertising. Starting at The York News-Times in York, Neb., Ahrens served as a graphic artist, retail sales representative and a member of the new media team. Ahrens worked as an advertising director for Lee Enterprises in its Lincoln, Neb., suburban business unit, as a publisher with the Omaha World Herald Co. in southwestern Iowa and with small market dailies and weeklies in the Midwest before he moved to Grand Forks in June 2010 as ad director. Ahrens has a bachelor's degree in speech communications with a minor in English from York College, York, Neb. In April 2013, Ahrens joined GateHouse Media Ohio as vice president, Sales.

"Powerful People Said, We Need Your Help"

Neil Brown, editor and vice president
The Tampa Bay Times
St. Petersburg, Fla.

I was a reporter at The Miami Herald in 1985. My assignment at the time was to cover the construction of Joe Robbie Stadium — a new stadium for the Miami Dolphins.

Joe Robbie, the owner of the Dolphins, wanted to build a stadium, and the county wanted to help him out because Miami Dolphins were such a force in the Miami area. So the county commission to help facilitate what Joe Robbie himself used to tout all the time as the only privately financed stadium in professional sports — the Dade County Commission gave him, for free, the land for the stadium, which was the only middle-class black neighborhood in Dade County, which always has had a very difficult relationship among the Anglo population, the Hispanic population and the black population. Of which the black population, in particular, felt voiceless.

So they get the area gifted to the county who then immediately turns it over, free, to Joe Robbie Stadium. The state then ponied up all kinds of state roadwork. It might've been a very good policy except for the homeowners in that particular area who felt very left out by the decision making.

In that middle-class neighborhood was Wilkie Ferguson and his wife, Betty Ferguson. Judge Wilkie Ferguson was the first-ever African American, state-appointed appellate judge in the state of Florida. He was a very prominent person, and his wife was a very prominent person. These were people of education, means and substance — who were fighting this.

As it turned out, the publisher of The Miami Herald at the time — Dick Capen — had endorsed the stadium. In fact, we had a model of the stadium on display in the lobby of The Miami Herald.

You learn there, among other things, the difference between the editorial board and the newspaper as a whole.

I wrote a lot of stories about the potential displacement of the black middle-class neighborhood in an area that didn't have many enclaves like this, and I remember Judge Ferguson and his wife came up to me saying, "Please don't stop your coverage. We can't shed the light."

They basically said to me, "Yeah, you may think we have some power, but you have no idea what kind of power The Miami Herald has."

I'd always worked for (former Herald city editor) John Brecher who used to say, "The reason to be in this business is to make the world a better place." That really captured it for me at a time when powerful people were saying to me, we need your help. Not just the voiceless people — who certainly, I understood, needed my help.

You said to yourself: Well, I knew I had to get it right. Now I really got to get it right.

HD video: http://www.whoneedsnewspapers.org/np_interviews.php?npId=epiphany&ivId=epiphany049

Neil Brown joined The Tampa Bay Times (formerly The St. Petersburg Times) in October 1993 as world editor overseeing national and international affairs. In May 2010, he was named editor and vice president. Before joining The Times, he served four years as managing editor of *Congressional Quarterly*, a weekly magazine devoted to national politics. Before joining CQ, he spent eight years as a reporter and editor at The Miami Herald, covering government and politics. Brown is a Phi Beta Kappa graduate of the University of Iowa and is a member of the journalism school's Hall of Fame. He is a member of the American Society of News Editors' Board of Directors and a past president and board member of the Florida Society of Newspaper Editors.

"It Helped Give Them a Voice"

Talibah Chikwendu, executive editor
The Afro-American
Baltimore, Md.

When I was working at my very first actual official reporting job at a daily, I had run across a woman who said her mother was having difficulty with getting her medical insurance to pay for something. She told me her story, and I wasn't sure it was a story. But I went and interviewed her mother. And when I talked to her mother — talked more to the family and started to really make some calls — I decided it really was a story. So I told her story.

The lady died now about five years ago, but to this day if that daughter sees me in the supermarket, she will thank me for telling her mother's story. If she's got her kids with her, she will say, "Remember. This was the lady who came." Because I made a difference for them.

I don't think the insurance company really resolved the issue the way they wanted, but they felt like there was a complete airing and that other people saw that there was an issue. It helped give them a voice to get just a little more from the insurance company than they were getting. And to this day [the daughter] still appreciates that.

So I would guess that this was the first time I realized that I could change things — by telling other people's stories. And that became really important for me.

HD video: http://www.whoneedsnewspapers.org/np_interviews.php?npld=epiphany&ivld=epiphany035

Talibah Chikwendu is the executive editor of the Afro-American Newspapers. She oversees the content production for the newspaper's three editions — Washington, Prince George's County and Baltimore — special publications and the website, AFRO.com.

Chikwendu has worked with The Afro for 13 years in a variety of positions including Baltimore editor, Washington editor, special publications editor, web editor, director of operations integration, radio show host and consultant.

Chikwendu is an award-winning columnist and photographer, with credits including The Baltimore Sun and Urban Influence, a publication of the National Urban League.

She has served on the Maryland-Delaware-District of Columbia Press Association's board of directors.

Chikwendu holds a bachelor of fine arts in digital design and a master's of business administration with a concentration in project management.

"None of Those Changes Would Have Happened without Us"

Suki Dardarian
Director, Audience Development/Innovation
The Seattle Times
Seattle, Wash.

I see the power and purpose every day. I see it in daily stories that we cover in which we clarify for readers what happened in that police incident or what happened in that public policy issue. I see it in the bigger, larger investigative pieces that we do.

The most recent investigative series we conducted was a project called "Seniors for Sale." It looked at how the adult family home business was putting seniors in this community at risk. Families were entrusting these homes with their parents and grandparents, and they were assured that they would be well taken care of in these homes. They were alternatives to nursing homes, they seemed homey, but, in fact, due to a variety of policy issues and business issues and other factors, countless, countless seniors were being poorly cared for. They were being put at risk, and in some cases they died — as a result of their poor care.

The stories that we heard from the community about the impact that investigation had on their families and their lives were huge. Folks sat down with us and shared their stories about the loss of their loved ones and in some cases their own feelings of guilt about that. They chose to sit down with us — they trusted us — and they told their stories. We were able to highlight areas for explanations of why this had come about. It had a huge impact on our community — from a family that's trying to decide where to put Mom, to legislation that's being worked on right now in our state legislature. None of those changes would have happened without us.

Nobody knew about these situations, but we have a great investigative team: an intrepid investigative reporter, who takes data and his own knowledge of this state and that industry and his fabulous way of sitting down and understanding people's lives and people's stories. He was able to pull all that together and, with the rest of the folks of the newsroom, deliver a powerful package of stories that we're all incredibly proud of and that made a huge impact on the community. I think our readers appreciate us for doing that.

HD video: http://www.whoneedsnewspapers.org/np_interviews.php?npId=epiphany &ivId=epiphany077

In March 2014, **Suki Dardarian** was named senior managing editor and vice president for the Minneapolis Star Tribune. Prior to that, Dardarian was one of two managing editors at The Seattle Times. In early 2011 she was appointed to oversee print and digital "curation" — editing, design and production — as well as seattletimes.com.

Dardarian joined The Times in 2000 as an assistant managing editor for metro news. She later became deputy managing editor and then managing editor, initially supervising news coverage — including local and business news, investigations, sports and features. She is a former president of the Associated Press Managing Editors, and she has served twice as a Pulitzer juror.

"We Really Got Beneath the Surface"

Rob Dean
(Former) Managing Editor
The Santa Fe New Mexican
Santa Fe, N.M.

About 10 years ago, when the town was flourishing economically, it was growing, and we saw that in Santa Fe the fastest-growing segment of the population was immigrant Hispanic. And what developed in Santa Fe was a very clear achievement gap.

It's become a common term now, but at that time it was not so common in schools. The gap between the achievement of established kids and students who were mostly minority, mostly poor — however you describe those segments demographically. In our case, it was very much ethnic — Anglo and Hispanic. That gap was evident, and it looked as though it was going to continue to grow. And indeed it has.

We took that piece of information and developed it into a significant long-term project. We laid it out for readers over a course of several days in a classic newspaper project. We really got beneath the surface and understood what were the sources of that achievement gap, and what were some strategies to overcome it. But, for that particular issue, we did more.

I worked in partnership with a local college and with a group of professionals to organize a community roundtable on the issue — a daylong forum of information and goal setting.

It was professionally facilitated, so, at the end of that day, we actually had a concrete set of goals.

We had earned — asked for and earned — a willingness to listen and receive our report from legislative leaders and the head of the State

Department of Education, all of whom attended the forum and participated in the last session.

It would be overstating the impact of that to say we got, right away, a dramatic reform in New Mexico, but that forum did inform a series or a package of legislation meant to tackle the achievement gap.

HD video: http://www.whoneedsnewspapers.org/np_interviews.php?npId=epiphany &ivId=epiphany063

After 21 years of service, **Rob Dean** retired from The Santa Fe New Mexican in July 2013. Before then, he worked at newspapers in Montana and Washington. A Montana native, he earned undergraduate degrees in journalism, history and politics from the University of Montana. He taught journalism at Pacific Lutheran University. Dean is past president of the New Mexico Foundation for Open Government and the Associated Press Managing Editors of New Mexico. He holds a master's degree in history from Norwich University in Vermont. In 2010, he edited the anthology "Santa Fe, Its 400th Year: Exploring the Past, Defining the Future," published by Sunstone Press.

"Why Don't You Go Do a Story on These Homeless People?"

Timothy Dwyer, executive editor
The Day
New London, Conn.

When I was working at The Boston Globe, I was still in college — hadn't graduated yet. To show how long ago this was, there was a homeless couple, and they were two of the first homeless people in Boston. They hung out on a corner on Huntington Avenue. It was such a big deal that the paper said, "Why don't you go do a story on these homeless people?" Because there just weren't any. They were either in shelters or they were in hospitals.

So I went and talked to them and did a story on the homeless couple.

The day the story appeared, the phones started ringing, and letters started coming, and, within a week, the homeless couple wasn't homeless anymore. They had an apartment — people sent cash in envelopes. Within a week, they had a place to live. That was the power of one little story. So that story was pretty much a bell-ringer for me.

HD video: http://www.whoneedsnewspapers.org/np_interviews.php?npld=epiphany&ivld=epiphany019

Timothy Dwyer became executive editor of The Day in July 2007. He began his career at The Boston Globe while a student at Northeastern University.

After seven years at The Globe covering everything from cops to politics, Dwyer joined the staff of The Philadelphia Inquirer.

He received the George Polk Award for national reporting, along with colleague Robert Frump, in 1983 for a series of investigative stories on the U.S. maritime industry. He served as deputy sports editor, a general sports columnist and sports editor. His work has appeared in The Best American Sports Writing anthology.

Dwyer has covered three Winter Olympics games, the World Series, the Super Bowl, the Stanley Cup Finals, the NBA playoffs, the NCAA basketball tournament, the Ryder Cup, the America's Cup and World Cup skiing.

After 20 years at The Inquirer, he became a metro reporter at The Washington Post. Dwyer covered President Bush's second inauguration, Hurricane Katrina, the Virginia Tech massacre and the trial of Zacarias Moussaoui.

"We Were Convinced That We Would Be Poor and Dead Last"

Lloyd Gray, executive editor
The Northeast Mississippi Daily Journal
Tupelo, Miss.

I was a capitol correspondent for several years for a paper on the Mississippi Gulf Coast — The Sun Herald. During that time, there was an almost continuous debate about improving education in Mississippi. We had just come through the trauma of school desegregation, and it could go either way in terms of whether we'd even consider that our public education system was worth saving.

The newspapers of Mississippi, including the one I work with, both in their coverage and in their editorials, raised the absolute urgent need of improvement of Mississippi's educational system. Basically the newspapers convinced the public of the necessity, and the public then convinced the legislature of the necessity.

We had a governor at the time who was very active in pushing for massive educational changes and reform — William Winter. And the newspapers were as responsible as any entity for the passage, in 1982, of the Mississippi Education Reform Act at a special session of the legislature.

The Clarion-Ledger, in Jackson, won a Pulitzer Prize for its role in that effort. It was, at that time, the most comprehensive educational reform effort in America. It was, for this state, more than just a policy decision or more than just the benefits of the legislation itself — which included tax increases. It included, for the first time, public kindergarten, mandatory school attendance, the beginnings of accountability and higher standards.

It was also — for Mississippi — a psychological breakthrough because, for so long, we had this inferiority complex. We were just convinced that we would always be poor and dead last in everything. And there wasn't really much we could do about it.

Newspapers rallied and convinced the people: We can be better. We can create a better future for our children. We can really think about creating a better life and prosperity in this state. Most newspapers in the state at that time were pretty much in lockstep, editorially, on this. So it was the power of a lot of newspapers. Maybe in this day and time, newspapers wouldn't have that reach or that power, but they did then.

There is no doubt in my mind that the newspaper that I worked for then and this newspaper, at that same time, had that impact.

HD video: http://www.whoneedsnewspapers.org/np_interviews.php?npld=epiphany &ivld=epiphany055

Lloyd Gray has worked for Mississippi newspapers since he was 16 years old, when he was hired as a part-time sportswriter at The Meridian Star. He has been executive editor of The Northeast Mississippi Daily Journal since 1992.

After graduation from Millsaps College in 1976, he interned at The Washington Post and then became a reporter for The Delta Democrat-Times in Greenville, Miss. He joined The Sun Herald in Biloxi in 1977, where he worked for 12 years as a reporter, capitol correspondent, managing editor and editorial page editor.

After a brief stint as a Mississippi assistant secretary of state, he became editor of his hometown paper, The Meridian Star, in 1990 before moving to Tupelo two years later. Gray is a past president of the Mississippi Press Association and a four-time winner of the state's top editorial writing award.

"In the Best Tradition of Newspapers — We Advocated"

Brian Greenspun, publisher and editor
The Las Vegas Sun
Las Vegas, Nev.

You pick any kind of major election in this state — The Las Vegas Sun has been a major, major player. We have taken candidates who had absolutely no chance of winning and supported them to the hilt, and they won. I can't tell you we're taking all the credit for that, but had we not — wrong people would've won, in my opinion. So you see the power of the media.

You also see the credibility of the media in terms of businesses that want to come to Las Vegas. They almost invariably come to the publisher's office to learn about the town. So it allows us to help sell the town.

They come to the newspaper because the perception is we know something about the town, and we have some influence in the town. Whether it's true or not is not the point — there is that perception.

Most recently, I'm not going to take credit for U.S. Sen. (Harry) Reid's victory, but everybody knows that he was in a very difficult race, and we pulled out all the stops, because we thought his reelection was absolutely essential to the future of the state, and we did what newspapers did in the best tradition of newspapers — we advocated.

Sen. Reid won, and we were a small part of that, but you knew you had some voice and some impact in that. You see it every single day. Mostly you see it in the little things. You see it in the regular lives of people who have nowhere else to go, who managed to make it to the newspaper where you can write the story or you can editorialize — you do the things newspapers can do or news organizations can do now.

For the most part, you get positive impacts. You see regular people's lives change dramatically. You see that every day. That's why I like this job.

HD video: http://www.whoneedsnewspapers.org/np_interviews.php?npld=epiphany &ivld=epiphany066

Brian Greenspun is publisher and editor of the Las Vegas Sun, founded by his father, Hank Greenspun, in 1950.

He is also chairman of the Greenspun Corporation, responsible for his family's business interests, which include real estate development (American Nevada Corporation), the city travel site (VEGAS.com), print and online publishing (Greenspun Media Group, the largest magazine publisher in Nevada) and luxury city magazines (Niche Media Holdings).

Greenspun has bachelor's and law degrees from Georgetown University, serves on the University of Nevada, Las Vegas Foundation and the Board of Trustees for The Brookings Institution.

"A 22-Year-Old Can Write a Story That Changes Someone's Life"

William (Bill) Hawkins
(Former) Publisher and Executive Editor
The Post and Courier
Charleston, S.C.

My first job as a full-time reporter was at The Harrisburg (Pa.) Patriot-News, and I was covering state government. I took an interest in state pensions, and dug in there, and I wrote a weeklong series on state pensions that basically turned the place upside down.

The outrage factor for what was going on — how the money was being lavishly spent and who benefited — raised holy hell.

I realized then the power of what I could do — one little, tiny reporter having all the major players in state government just absolutely frazzled. That power is still out there in our newsrooms today, and we've seen it here.

Reporting has forced changes in code. It has forced changes in how children are taught. It's forced changes in how public money is spent. It's forced changes in how reporting on open government is done.

We're involved in a major lawsuit now. We'll still spend money suing to get access to public records — to get access to information that clearly ought to be in the public domain — that hasn't changed. A 22-year-old kid can go out there and write a story that changes someone's life. That's still the power and the glory of this job.

HD video: http://www.whoneedsnewspapers.org/np_interviews.php?npld=epiphany&ivld=epiphany043

Bill Hawkins came to The Post and Courier as executive editor in 2005, from Durham, N.C., where he spent 17 years as executive editor and vice president of The Herald-Sun. He was named publisher of The Post and Courier in 2009 and in that capacity was also responsible for advertising, circulation and the web. He retired from The Post and Courier in July 2012.

Hawkins is a graduate of Cornell University and earned a Bronze Star as an intelligence officer with the 11th Infantry Brigade in Vietnam.

"The Value of Writing Something Down and Sharing It"

Mike Jacobs, retired publisher
The Grand Forks Herald
Grand Forks, N.D.

There was a controversy in Dickinson, (N.D.) between the city council and the county commission. They had a joint meeting that I covered. The city people had brought their zoning ordinances. The county people had — this is typical — they had just, sort of — come. So I wrote a little story about how one side was prepared and the other side wasn't. No agreement could be reached.

So, in the morning, the county commission chairman called, and said, "We're having another meeting, and I'm bringing my books."

I thought: That's happening because I pointed out they had made a critical mistake. They didn't come prepared, so the city had an advantage over them that shouldn't have happened, and they recognized that after they read it in the paper.

I had the same sort of thing happen this weekend. I wrote a column about the [University of North Dakota] Fighting Sioux controversy, and I got an email early Sunday morning from a woman that said, "Thank you, for that. Now I understand where people are coming from." It's just the value of writing something down and sharing it.

God knows, like every newspaper editor, I get more criticism than praise. But it's always gratifying in either event because it shows me that people do take the newspaper seriously.

HD video: http://www.whoneedsnewspapers.org/np_interviews.php?npld=epiphany&ivld=epiphany100

Mike Jacobs retired as publisher of The Grand Forks Herald in March 2014. He was appointed editor of The Grand Forks Herald in 1984 and editor and publisher in 2004. Jacobs grew up milking cows near Stanley, N.D., graduated from the University of North Dakota and has worked as a farm laborer and a bartender. Jacobs' career in newspapers includes stops in Dickinson, Mandan and Fargo, N.D. The Herald won the Pulitzer Prize for Public Service after the Red River flood of 1997. Jacobs was named editor of the year and won ASNE's distinguished writing award for his flood-related editorials.

"People Take Action Based on Our Reporting"

Mike Knaak
Assistant Managing Editor
The St. Cloud Times
St. Cloud, Minn.

These things happen fairly regularly. You write a story and something changes and people react to it.

I did quite a bit of coverage, in the '70s and early '80s, on the effort to build and the actual building of a high-voltage power line through Western Minnesota. The story was widely covered by lots of media.

We were perhaps the most thorough and most consistent journalists on that story, and that story still shapes people's lives. People are concerned about the routing and health issues of power lines.

That story, because it was such a big deal, and had so much impact on so many people, it made me realize that what we do is important — because people take action based on our reporting. They shape some of their actions based on our reporting and really care about what we tell them. They depend on what we tell them.

What we do matters. What we do sometimes shapes how people react and how they vote. People are paying attention to what we're doing. It's not just sort of an "exercise."

HD video: http://www.whoneedsnewspapers.org/np_interviews.php?npld=epiphany &ivld=epiphany097

Mike Knaak is responsible for news content in Times Media's family of websites, breaking news coverage online and in print, photos, multimedia and newsroom systems. Knaak also works with reporters on computer-assisted reporting enterprise reports. Knaak has worked at The Times since 1975 in a variety of jobs including regional news editor, photo and graphics editor, assignment editor and systems editor. Knaak is a former president of the Minnesota Pro Chapter of the Society of Professional Journalists. He is an adjunct faculty member at St. Cloud State. He graduated from St. Cloud State in 1975 with a bachelor of arts degree.

"It Had Been, Essentially, Swept Under the Carpet"

Darel LaPrade
Senior V.P., New Media Independent Newspapers
The Delaware State News
Dover, Del.

I was the editor of a weekly newspaper on the Outer Banks of North Carolina, and it was in late July, and the roads were clotted with traffic, and the temperature was near 100, and we were struggling to get that week's issue out the door, trying to cover everything that needed to be covered.

And this woman walked in — whom I did not know, which was very odd for me because I knew everyone in the community.

She came in, and she was perspiring, she was hot, she was exhausted, and she said, "I'm going to have to close the domestic violence shelter because I can't pay my electric bill. I don't have air conditioning, and I cannot keep it open." It was a good cause, and there were women who were suffering — that needed the shelter.

To make a long story short, the newspaper produced a series of stories about the problem of domestic violence in the small community. [Stories about] how it had been, essentially, swept under the carpet, and the role that this shelter played in the life of the community in saving these women.

Within about three weeks or four weeks, we had the shelter back on firm financial footing. We had a new board of directors in place. And there was all sorts of "whohah" that took place. It was just that moment when I understood what journalism was all about.

HD video: http://www.whoneedsnewspapers.org/np_interviews.php?npld=epiphany
&ivld=epiphany029

Darel LaPrade is a publisher and senior V.P. new media for Independent Newspapers. He started with Independent as a special projects manager and group
advertising director for Delmarva, Del., in 1996. In 1997, he became V.P. advertising,
a position he held until 2005 when he was named V.P. operations and in 2006
V.P. corporate operations. In 2007, he assumed responsibility for the company's
new media operations and in 2010 became publisher of five weekly newspapers
in Delaware and Maryland. His 30-year newspaper career includes a stint with
The Virginian-Pilot in Norfolk, Va., where he first worked as a district circulation
manager. He also served as an editor, group V.P. and corporate general manager
for Atlantic Publications, Inc., which once published 24 community resort weeklies
in Maryland, Virginia, North Carolina, and South Carolina.

"A Really Good Reminder of Why I Got Into the Business"

Tim Lott
(Former) V.P. Audience Strategy
The Austin American-Statesman
Austin, Texas

I had done a year as a copy editor on the sports desk, and I was anxious to get back to reporting, so I became the San Marcos [Texas] Bureau, which was my apartment in San Marcos — it's a college town.

There was a fire on the edge of San Marcos — right at the edge of the city limits as you get into the unincorporated county out in the country. Two kids died in this fire, and some reporting that I did uncovered the fact that firefighters, on the scene — one crew from the city, one crew from a volunteer fire department that was at the county level — actually, literally, physically fought over who would get to put the fire out. And while they fought — two kids died. It was just outrageous on its face.

Not that you don't understand that the volunteer fire fighters constantly need to improve their skills, but there was a territorialism — two government agencies, literally fighting — while the children in the house died.

Now, I think, conceivably, the kids in the house could've been dead already, but the point that firefighters were fighting over who gets the glory of putting out a fire while kids died — it was just outrageous.

Reporting that was a really good reminder of why I got into the business — because that kind of thing shouldn't happen. To me — that's newspaper work at its best.

HD video: http://www.whoneedsnewspapers.org/np_interviews.php?npld=epiphany &ivld=epiphany059

Tim Lott is vice president Disruptive Innovation, Cox Media Group. Previously, Lott was vice president for audience strategy at The Austin American-Statesman, where he oversaw the newspaper's efforts to develop nontraditional revenue streams. In 2011, the newspaper launched both a paid sports site focusing on the Texas Longhorns and a streaming radio station. Prior to his current position, Lott was VP/digital. Lott has held numerous reporting and editing positions at The American-Statesman, where he began working in 1989. Prior to that, he worked for the Associated Press. Lott is a graduate of Baylor University.

"This Is Something That Can Really Change Lives"

Ray Marcano, director
Digital Audience Growth
Cox Media Group
Dayton, Ohio

When I was health and medical reporter, a source of mine told me that the local children's hospital was not sending babies to a local [general] hospital for treatment, but would instead send them, via helicopter, to another children's hospital — hundreds of miles away. Some babies had died in transport, and I wrote about that.

I talked to everybody involved. I had a source who gave me memos, detailing what was going on. There was a civil lawsuit involved that I covered — all of that.

At the end of the day, the children's hospital finally stopped that practice. They finally started sending babies to the local hospital that could do the same care. When that happened, that's when that light went [on].

Because it was like not only was this a fantastic story — forget for a second that that was a fantastic story — but at some point there is going to be a baby that got to the local hospital just in the nick of time and was saved instead of having to be put on a helicopter and transported hundreds of miles away.

That was a time that the light went [on], and I went, "Boy, this is something that can really change lives."

HD video: http://www.whoneedsnewspapers.org/np_interviews.php?npld=epiphany &ivld=epiphany002

Ray Marcano was named director of Digital Audience Growth for Cox Media Group, Ohio, in August 2013. He began his career at Westchester Rockland Newspapers in White Plains, N.Y., and he also worked at a small weekly in his hometown of New York City. He worked at two newspapers in Oklahoma, including The Tulsa World, before coming to the Dayton Daily News. In Dayton, he's held a number of reporting and management jobs including sports editor, metro editor, regional editor, deputy managing editor and Internet general manager. He is a former national president of the Society of Professional Journalists and is a two-time Pulitzer Prize juror. His website, www.RayMarcano.com, keeps those interested in digital media up to date on the latest trends.

"The Huge Risks They Were Taking Struck Me as What Journalism Was About"

Richard Meeker, publisher and co-owner
Willamette Week
Portland, Ore.

I'll give you a large example that probably really did influence me, although it's probably almost trite. Then a smaller example that is more realistic about what we really do.

I grew up in Washington, D.C.; I read The Washington Post and The New York Times at the breakfast table from as early as I could read. Through my friend, Bill Graham, I was close to the Washington Post Co., and there were the Pentagon Papers and Watergate. I actually even got to sit in on court hearings and visit the Graham household during these times. I got to watch how, especially Mrs. Graham, played with these huge issues.

I think something about seeing ordinary humans — Kay Graham was a pretty significant person — but seeing human beings dealing with these earthshaking issues in a calm, coherent fashion and actually having fun while they were at it, shaped me.

I watched Mrs. Graham and Nicholas von Hoffman have an argument about a column he wrote about Watergate. The huge risks that they were taking struck me as what journalism was about and didn't strike me as risks. The Deep Throat business, and all that, struck me as legitimate journalism and not as risky. All this stuff about Kay Graham is "gonna get her tit caught in a big fat wringer" — I never feared for her.

So those two journalistic activities that involved competing newspapers — The Times and The Post — highlighted the way the world works, and how things are nowhere near so simple as you might think them, and showed journalism changing the course of the world.

Now, that's the big example. I had nothing to do with it; I was just a spectator.

Once upon a time, there was a battle in this town about guidelines for upgrading class-B buildings. The building owners did not want to install bike racks or leave any space for bicycles. Willamette Week wrote an article about this big (*indicates about two inches*) about recalcitrant building owners. The day that issue of the paper came out — the issue of the bike racks went away.

There are bike racks in every class-B building in town, and that's not why we are such a bicycle-friendly community today, but without things like that, early on, it would be harder to be a bicycle-friendly community. One little article in our paper — period ... the end — changed the debate. And we didn't even think it would.

HD video: http://www.whoneedsnewspapers.org/np_interviews.php?npld=epiphany &ivld=epiphany073

Richard Meeker has been Willamette Week's publisher since 1983, when he and Editor Mark Zusman formed City of Roses Newspaper Company to purchase the paper from the Eugene Register-Guard. Meeker started with the paper as a reporter at its founding in 1974 and became editor in 1977. Meeker is a graduate of Amherst College and the University of Oregon School of Law. He taught school for one year on Ocracoke Island on the Outer Banks of North Carolina. He grew up in Washington, D.C., where he got his start in newspapers in the seventh grade. Meeker is married to Ellen Rosenblum, a judge on the Oregon Court of Appeals. He and his wife have two children — Cate and Will.

"We Had Made a Difference"

John Winn Miller, publisher
The Concord Monitor
Concord, N.H.

When I was a reporter in Kentucky, the State Supreme Court declared the education system unconstitutional. My newspaper — The Lexington Herald-Leader under John Carroll, who went on to The Baltimore Sun and The LA Times — did a series of stories. We dedicated 10 reporters for six months, traveling throughout the poorer parts of Kentucky, looking at not the obvious stories about how bad education was, but the not-so-obvious stories about why it was, and who was really cheating the children of Kentucky by the way they were financing education — by the special favors that property tax assessors were doing for very wealthy people.

We came up with a series of stories that literally changed thousands of lives in Kentucky. Because, as a result (partially, not entirely) of what we did, the legislature passed a massive tax increase — the largest tax increase in the state's history. They passed education reform that dramatically restructured the way funding was done for education in Kentucky that held teachers and schools accountable for the first time — legislation that balanced the poor counties in Eastern Kentucky, in particular, with the wealthier counties in the central part of the state.

The reaction we got from readers was astounding — that we made a difference in their lives. We made a difference in their children's lives. And — from legislators to school kids — we heard. That was when we truly understood that we had made a difference, and a difference that will last a long, long time.

HD video: http://www.whoneedsnewspapers.org/np_interviews.php?npld=epiphany&ivld=epiphany011

John Winn Miller joined Newspapers of New England as publisher of The Concord Monitor in September 2010. Miller started his career as a magazine reporter in Louisville, Ky., and then joined the Associated Press, which he worked for in Louisville, New York and Rome. He briefly served as Rome bureau chief of The Wall Street Journal/Europe before returning to his hometown to work for The Lexington Herald-Leader. He was part of a team of reporters whose prize-winning series on education in Kentucky helped lead to major reform. Miller then served as editor at The Centre Daily Times in State College, Pa., The Tallahassee Democrat, and publisher of The Olympian in Olympia, Wash.

"Being a Part of Something That Keeps an Eye on Things"

Sean Oates, web editor
The Record
Woodland, Park, N.J.

I worked on the (Ramapo River, Ringwood, N.J.) "Toxic Legacy" project. It carries a lot of meaning for me to this day and reminds me of why I'm involved in something as crazy as covering the news. There is something about changing the status quo by simply shedding light on information that can make a huge difference in people's lives.

It became clear to me, in the aftermath of what we had published, that the folks who lived among the polluted sites were now being noticed. In some cases they were getting health care paid for and were getting assistance, and their stories were being heard. That really brought it home for me.

After I moved on from this company and tried something different, which I had done for many reasons — living in California and working in a role which was basically to cultivate pop-culture video — red carpets and artist interviews and musicians and all the fun stuff I thought I was missing out on. I found that I missed the element of true local impact.

There's something about coming back to the place I grew up, and every day being a part of something that keeps an eye on things — that you can't beat with all the glitz and glamour in the world.

So a combination of having worked on some great projects like the pollution project, and then having worked on the other side of the business on the other side of the country — that really gels for me why I'm drawn to this kind of work.

HD video: http://www.whoneedsnewspapers.org/np_interviews.php?npld=epiphany &ivld=epiphany026

Sean Oates is the web editor at NorthJersey.com, the news site for North Jersey Media Group's family of newspapers, including The Record and The Herald News daily publications. The site attracts 1.7 million monthly unique visitors. Born and raised in Bergen County, N.J., Sean graduated from Ramapo College in 2000.

"That [Picture] Changed My Life"

John J. "Jake" Oliver, CEO and publisher
The Afro-American
Baltimore, Md.

When I was a kid, my father — who was the president of this paper with his cousin who was the chairman and his other cousins who were all around him when he retired — as president, he had an old-world perspective of what this paper was supposed to be about.

When I was 5, 6 or 7 years old, I couldn't understand: Why is this paper called Afro? Why are we only writing about black people? I don't understand, and I don't like it — until ...

[The editor], Carl Murphy, ran a picture of Emmett Till on the front page. That [picture] changed my life. I just had to look at that — for hours. I couldn't understand how any human being could do that to another human being. Then, it dawned on me: Racism. Hatred. And, suddenly, I realized why we had The Afro.

HD video: http://www.whoneedsnewspapers.org/np_interviews.php?npld=epiphany &ivld=epiphany035

John "Jake" Oliver holds a B.A. degree from Fisk University in Nashville, Tenn. (1969), and a J.D. degree from the Columbia University School of Law, New York, N.Y. (1972). He is a member of both the New York and Maryland bars. Oliver served two terms (1999–2003) as President of the National Newspaper Publishers Association (NNPA), the trade organization for publishers of Black owned and operated newspapers in the U.S. He also served as president of the Maryland-D.C.-Delaware Press Association. Oliver was the Chairman of the Maryland Higher Education Commission, which provides curriculum and financial oversite of all the higher education institutions in Maryland. Oliver is a life member of the NAACP and the Kappa Alpha Psi Fraternity. For the past nine years, Oliver has been a participant in the Media Focus Group of the Aspen Institute in Aspen, Colo.

"A Very Positive Impact on the Community"

Kevin Olson, associate publisher
The Jackson Hole News & Guide
Jackson, Wyo.

My aha moment — that displayed the impact of journalism and publishing — was around the year 2000. I worked for The Orange County Register at the time, and we really worked hard to make the community come alive through this momentous occasion — the turn-of-the-century, 2000.

We set out on a very ambitious publishing project where we told the history of Orange County. We made the history come alive in classrooms through a mobile education program. We had magazines that focused on different facets of our life in that community.

The newspaper had a series of stories over the course of a year that allowed our residents to really see the fabric of life in that community. What the community got as a result of that project was a real clear understanding of what made the county great — what its struggles were and what its successes were. What the children could look forward to in its future; what their role in the future was.

That was a shining moment that showed how the sum of all the efforts of what you do as a publisher can really come out and make a community understand where it's at and where it needs to go.

As we transition to Jackson Hole, I feel a similar project is this Jackson Hole Compass Project that we're doing.

It really allows the residents to know where we're headed as a community, and what our individual roles can be in preserving what we like — or changing what we don't like. We — as a news organization — spur on that effort through what we do. Some people will say, "Well, all you guys do is write on the bad news." Well, the flip side of that would be:

Through revealing some of the bad stuff, we understand what it takes to get better. I think that's a moral compass that's very important for a community.

HD video: http://www.whoneedsnewspapers.org/np_interviews.php?npld=epiphany &ivld=epiphany083

Kevin Olson began his publishing career and held a variety of sales and marketing positions with The Orange County Register in Santa Ana, Calif. He is a gracuate of the Walter Cronkite School of Journalism and Telecommunications at Arizona State University in Tempe, Ariz. His professional background includes sales management, hotel/resort/tourism advertising, sponsorship development/acquisition and publication product development. Aside from his professional responsibilities, Kevin is an avid skier, cyclist, golfer and family activities planner.

"Hey, You Know What? This Isn't Right!"

James W. (Jim) Rainey
Publisher, The Opelika-Auburn News
Opelika, Ala.

I was a reporter, early on, in the AIDS epidemic, covering some of that. Again, this was in West Tennessee. I went to live for a couple of weeks with a young couple, with children, who were dying. They were in the later stages of AIDS. It was right around Christmas time.

One of the things that we did in our reporting was that we found that a great deal of the funding for AIDS education had taken place in major metro areas, but that the federal government was not spending any money, almost, in the rural areas.

This couple suffered a great deal of discrimination — a really horrific time for them — and had been kicked out of their church; their kids had been ostracized and picked on at school. Through reporting on what happened with them — the lack of funding and the lack of education — the region decided that: Hey, you know what? This isn't right! These people are not being treated with the care and kindness that they deserve, and there are many others out there.

It really exposed how far-reaching this epidemic really was, and that it was growing, and that it was growing in their midst. People were really ignorant of that fact. When the light of day was shined down upon that, it led to a real reaction not only of local governments but local churches, local citizen leaders who stepped up to the plate, and it led to a real change throughout that region of Tennessee. That really made me feel like what we were doing really mattered.

HD video: http://www.whoneedsnewspapers.org/np_interviews.php?npId=epiphany &ivId=epiphany051

Jim Rainey has been publisher of The Opelika-Auburn News since December 2002. He also serves as news leader for Media General newspapers, television stations and affiliated websites in the Gulf South Region. Since 2002, The News has won the Alabama Press Association's General Excellence Award six of the past seven years. In 2006, the *Newspaper Association of America's Presstime Magazine* named Rainey one of the nation's top 20 newspaper professionals under the age of 40. Rainey came to Lee County from Atlanta, where he was associate publisher of The Fulton County Daily Report, an American Lawyer Media publication.

"Nobody Else Could Have Done That Type of Work"

Zach Ryall, online managing editor
The Austin American-Statesman
Austin, Texas

Some of the most powerful journalism that, I think, we've produced has had to do with both watchdog reporting as well as just great enterprise reporting.

I recall a visual piece and word piece that we produced some years ago about a young woman named Jacqueline Saburido — who was a young Venezuelan U.T. [University of Texas] student who had been involved in a very, very tragic accident, involving a drunk driver on one of the winding roads just west of town. She was horribly burned in that accident and horribly disfigured and thought dead and was not. We first became aware of her when we were covering the trial of the drunk driver that hit her.

One of our photographers — Rodolfo Gonzalez — who still works for the American-Statesman — and a reporter — who is not with us any longer — decided they wanted to chronicle both the trial and her recovery, which was a very, very long painful recovery. So out of that body of work was produced a multi-page spread of stunning photographs that documented her, and the relationship she had with her father and mother, and the relationship she developed with the young man who hit her — who served prison time.

I recall when that work was produced, feeling just incredibly proud of what we do. How nobody else could have done that type of work — except a newspaper. A newspaper that was willing to dedicate the time, resources and newsprint into that type of story.

So what did it change? It immediately was seized upon as a national story. Jacqueline Saburido went on to become a spokesperson for Mothers

Against Drunk Driving and donated a lot of her time and our images and her story to campaigning against drunk driving. And that campaign still goes on today. Part of that was because of the piece that Rodolfo and his writing partner produced and The Statesman's commitment to telling that type of story in the depth that we did.

HD video: http://www.whoneedsnewspapers.org/np_interviews.php?npld=epiphany &ivld=epiphany060

Zach Ryall is a 1976 graduate of the University of Texas journalism program and has been working for The Austin American-Statesman for 34 years. He started his professional career with The Statesman, shooting Friday night football, and soon he became a full-time staff photographer. After 10 years of shooting, he became the director of photography, managing the visual report and the transition from chemicals and film to the digital world. Since 2008, Ryall has served as the online managing editor for statesman.com and austin360.com, the news and entertainment websites of The Statesman.

"I'm the Conveyor Belt"

Mike Townsend, executive editor
The Burlington Free Press
Burlington, Vt.

What I find, as I developed over the years, is that the word objective is not the right word. I am this absorption board, OK? I absorb everything around me no matter what your perspective is.

No matter how kooky or wacky or far out you may be in terms of your message, I've learned, over the years, just to listen for a little bit — and I'm fairly quick in weeding out the wackiness. But sometimes, it takes a little while for people to give you that message.

This is a very dynamic community in terms of age, background, politics, our closeness to Montréal — you've got Socialists here, Communists, the whole bit. I've really grown attached to these individuals and their perspectives and understanding the dynamic of what brings a community together and makes it work.

I think the most valuable thing I've learned is that I'm the conveyor belt. You may not see me as an ally on the editorial page when I poke you in the eye with an editorial, but I'm going to always say, "If you come back and say I want space. I'm going to give it to you." I make sure that there's a level playing field in all the platforms.

When I write something and I get the tar beat out of me, online, from chat rooms, I have a friend, she'll say, "They're really being unfair." I say, "Well, I own the platform. I own the print platform, and I own the online. I am the 300-pound gorilla. My job is to make sure that it's shared with everybody." If they really need to beat me up, I just let them do it. That's because that's the way they feel like they're getting their comeuppance.

That really plays out in all facets. It doesn't just have to be the political field. It's also in any other area where people need to get their information out. We have actually seen when we put something in print and online — your chances of getting attendance are far better if you give it to the newspaper than somebody else. So you see that influence — right away.

HD video: http://www.whoneedsnewspapers.org/np_interviews.php?npld=epiphany &ivld=epiphany009

Mike Townsend is a graduate of the University of Maryland, College of Journalism. He began his career as a reporter for two scrub weeklies, The Carroll Record and The Sykesville Herald, but reported for only a short time. He moved quickly into editing as editor, The Carroll County Times in Westminster, Md.; suburban editor, The Harford Sun, an edition of The (Baltimore) Sun; managing editor, The Rockford (Ill.) Register Star; executive editor, The Marin (Calif.) Independent Journal; and managing editor, The Des Moines (Iowa) Register. Townsend is now executive editor of the Burlington Free Press in what he describes as picture-perfect Vermont where he walks to work every day and rides a Trek up to 100 miles on weekends.

"No Other Newspaper Would Listen to Her"

Wendy Warren
(Former) V.P. and Editor, Philly.com
The Philadelphia Daily News
Philadelphia, Pa.

When I was in college, we still pasted up the college newspaper with hot wax and X-Acto knives, and had blue pens and all that good stuff.

I remember hearing stories that the Student Government Association would meet in secret, and we would write about that. Then they would have to open up the meetings, because it was clearly a violation of the state's law. That kind of early work was very impressive to me.

But probably the times I felt it the most has been at The Daily News when The Daily News would write a story about somebody who would never, ever, ever, get their story told.

Jill Porter — a wonderful columnist, now retired from The Daily News — wrote a series of stories about this grandmother — I think she lived in West Philly — a poorly educated and poor woman, but a proud woman who came home from a hospital stay and found that her possessions and her house had been moved out to the curb, and someone else was living in her house.

It turned out someone had gone down to the Recorder of Deeds office and simply filed a transfer of [her] deed for a dollar and had stolen this woman's house. That woman — her name was Devota Clark — that woman's story, when we published it, we were amazed to find that it was by no means an isolated incident, and that lots of people in Philadelphia had their house stolen from them with these deed scams.

There were some changes that could be made in the Recorder of Deeds office that would make a difference. There were changes that could be made to the notary system that would make a difference. Jill started writing about this, and those changes were made.

Something as simple as a postcard was instituted where [when] someone walks into the Recorder of Deeds office and tries to switch a deed, they sent a postcard to the house owner. And suddenly we found out that people were stealing houses.

There was a criminal investigation; there were charges. It was a wonderful moment for this woman, who I know nobody else would listen to — nobody but The Daily News. No other paper would listen to her because it sounded so crazy — and she was right.

HD video: http://www.whoneedsnewspapers.org/np_interviews.php?npld=epiphany &ivld=epiphany006

Wendy Warren joined NBC Washington as editorial manager, digital, in September 2012. Previously, she was the editor and vice president of Philly.com, which produces original video and online content and showcases the work of the city's two daily newspapers, The Philadelphia Daily News and The Philadelphia Inquirer.

Prior to being named to her Philly.com role in May 2008, Warren was an assistant managing editor at The Philadelphia Daily News. She ran the newspaper's news and online operations, including The Daily News' multimedia project covering the 2007 Philadelphia mayoral race, award-winning projects ranging from exposure of massive corruption in the city's parking ticket office to coverage of the state takeover of city schools, and for eight years, she produced the newspaper's "Rethinking Philadelphia" project, which called citizens together to push the city to innovate and improve.

Prior to joining The Daily News in 2000, Warren was the business editor and a business writer at The Morning Call in Allentown, Pa., where she was named a Times-Mirror Journalist of the Year in 1998.

"They're Going to Bring in Alligators?"

Scott Wasser
(Former) Executive Editor
The Portland Press Herald
Portland, Maine

In the days when there was no email, you had to make photocopies of your few articles, and then you had to put a stamp on the envelope. I sent out 186.

The only job offering I got was in Stuttgart, Ark. — a tiny little town of about 10,000 or 12,000. The newspaper was about 3,000–4,000 circulation. I went.

I had just gotten engaged at the time, left my fiancé behind and drove to Stuttgart, Ark. It was as big a culture shock as you can imagine.

One of my responsibilities was covering the Fish and Game Commission. I went out with one of the commissioners to fly over the forests in Arkansas looking for forest fires. While we were up there, we talked about various things, and one was trying to control the beaver population. The part of Arkansas that I lived in was a big rice- and soybean-producing area, and what they did depended on irrigation and flooding of crops — controlling water.

There was also a huge beaver population that made that difficult. The beavers were constantly a problem. They were being trapped and hunted, but it was not controlling the population. So one of the things they thought they would try to do to control the beavers was to bring in alligators from Louisiana. The beavers didn't have any natural predators, but the alligators would be a natural predator and eliminate the beavers.

The commissioner's telling me all this, and I'm thinking: They're going to bring in alligators? As a New York boy standing in Stuttgart, Ark., the only time I'd ever seen an alligator was on the movie screen. It struck me that if I were a farmer the last thing I'd want to be doing is wading through my fields in hip waders, not knowing if there was an alligator under the water — especially an alligator that had just eaten every beaver in sight.

So I said, "Now wait a second. If you have a beaver population that has no natural predators, and you bring in alligators, isn't that going to pose a greater problem than the beavers do now to the farmers?"

He looked at me, and he said, "Jeez, we hadn't thought about that, but I guess we'll have to deal with it when the time comes."

I wrote a column on it, and I said this is unbelievable.

I don't know that that article ever did anything, but as far as I know there are no alligators in that part of Arkansas today. I got a lot of feedback, and it opened eyes that had no idea this was going on.

That was probably the first time that I did anything — in the way of reporting or writing — that I saw a direct impact, or at least what I thought was a direct impact, on society.

HD video: http://www.whoneedsnewspapers.org/np_interviews.php?npId=epiphany&ivId=epiphany014

Scott Wasser was vice president and executive editor of MaineToday Media's The Portland Press Herald and Maine Sunday Telegram from 2009 to 2012. Previously, Wasser was managing editor and vice president for news at The Times Leader in Wilkes-Barre, Pa. In addition to his managerial duties, Wasser periodically writes a car column and has contributed articles to Road & Track and Open Road magazines and USA Today.

"The Responsibility of What We Do"

Mark Zusman, editor and co-owner
Willamette Week
Portland, Ore.

We did a story last year about a standing U. S. senator who is one of the wealthiest senators in Washington whose fortune was made because he's either the largest, or one of the largest, frozen pea processors in America. One of his positions in DC has been fairly harsh on the issue of illegal immigration. We sent a reporter who speaks Spanish out to his processing plant, which is in Pendleton, Ore. She speaks Spanish. We wrote a story about how a large number of his workers are undocumented workers.

We did [another] story many years ago about a middle school in Portland that was poisoning its kids and its teachers for years, and these reports were available and no one was paying any attention to them. A reporter put together the story; the next day the school shut down. It has never reopened. The story that we did ... about the tax code in America, which has been picked up by Reuters, by the Columbia Journalism Review, and was even featured on Rachel Maddow ... I can't say it's changed the debate about taxes, but it's helped.

I could go on and on. On a regular basis I am reminded both of the responsibility of what we do and the power of what we do, even in this small little corner of the world.

HD video: http://www.whoneedsnewspapers.org/np_interviews.php?npld=epiphany&ivld=epiphany074

Mark Zusman is the editor and co-owner of Willamette Week and The Santa Fe Reporter. Zusman has been editor of Willamette Week for 26 years. In 1986, Zusman was awarded the Gerald Loeb award for Business Journalism for an article he did about Nike. Zusman is a past-president of the board of the Independent Media Institute and the board of the Association of Alternative Newsweeklies. He serves as a judge for the Payne Award for Ethics in Journalism. He has taught journalism at the University of Oregon and lectured at the Academy of Alternative Journalism at the Medill School of Journalism at Northwestern University. He is also a former fellow of the East-West Center.

Section III

SERVING COMMUNITY

The ⬤ Day

OUR MISSION

To publish the highest quality newspaper and to be the dominant source of news and advertising in the region.

To be a strong, profitable company that serves the needs of the customer.

To be a good employer.

To lead in the growth and well-being of the region.

To return the company's profits to the community to serve the public interest.

"*The newspaper should be more than a business enterprise. It should also be the champion and protector of the public interest and defender of the people's rights.*"

— As written by Theodore Bodenwein, owner and publisher of The Day from 1891-1939, in his will establishing The Day Trust.

Serving Community

"A newspaper should be more than a business enterprise. It should also be the champion and protector of the public interest and defender of the people's rights."
— *Thedore Bodenwein, owner and publisher of* The Day, *1891–1939*
From his will, establishing the Day Trust, 1939

To Jim Mayo, publisher of The Sequoyah Times, Sallisaw, Okla., his semi-weekly newspaper is "the glue that helps hold [this community] together." What would happen to his town if its newspaper closed? "Well, if you take out the glue, it disintegrates," says Mayo.

Their language is not often as plain and apocalyptic, but editors and publishers of the 50 newspapers we visited in our reporting expedition across the U.S.A. concur with Mayo. Many describe their newspapers as the forum where community ideas and events are documented and shared — its marketplace of ideas.

"A good newspaper is like a community talking to itself," says John Bodette, editor of The St. Cloud Times, St. Cloud, Minn.

Local newspapers conceive of themselves as the watchdogs of their communities, the facilitators of community conversation and commerce, and the stenographers writing the first draft of their community's history.

In this section, professional journalists share personal epiphanies about how they recognized this community-building mission.

"A Journalistically Religious Experience"

David Boardman
(Former) Executive Editor
The Seattle Times
Seattle, Wash.

We had a pretty horrendous ice and snowstorm here — we don't get a lot of snow in the wintertime — and the power was knocked out for several days, and it was unusually cold. We have a fairly large and growing immigrant community — many of those people come from much warmer climates.

One night there was a family of Vietnamese immigrants — middle-class, relatively well-to-do immigrant family — who lived in the suburb of Bellevue in a large four-bedroom home. Their power was out, and they were cold. They brought their charcoal grill inside the house to warm up the house. And all — I believe it was — all six members of the family perished from the fumes. I was just deeply troubled by that, as a lot of people were, and worked on the story here before I left for the evening, and went home and really felt deeply moved by what had happened.

I woke up the next morning — and it's as close as I ever had to a journalistically religious experience — my alarm went off at 5:30, as it does every morning, and I popped out of bed with a fully formed vision of what I wanted the front page to look like that day. I went into the shower with a glass door, and I'm drawing this out on the door, so I don't forget it. I rushed into the office, and what we decided to do was based on this vision I had.

We consulted King County, and we found what were the most commonly used foreign languages in this county. We dedicated the entire top half of our front page to do — in very large and very red letters, in those five, most commonly used foreign languages — a warning to people not to do what these people had done: Not to burn charcoal or gas grills in their home. Now, that's not something a lot of newspapers would do because it's not a good way to sell newspapers to your English-speaking customers. But our feeling was: If some Somali immigrant is in the 7-Eleven, buying milk and cigarettes, and sees his or her language popping up from the newsstand, they're going to pay attention, and we might be able to save a life or two.

We dedicated our whole front page to it, and we heard back afterward from many community groups that it really got people talking — it got people's attention. It prevented people from that practice, and most importantly it said to those new Americans: "Wow! This is what a newspaper does. And wasn't this something? They were willing to sacrifice some money in order to give us a warning." To me, that was really a graphic example of what we do — and nobody else does.

HD video: http://www.whoneedsnewspapers.org/np_interviews.php?npld=epiphany &ivld=epiphany076

David Boardman was named dean of Temple University's School of Media and Communication in July 2013. Previously, Boardman was executive editor and senior vice president of The Seattle Times, with oversight and responsibility for the news department and seattletimes.com. Under his leadership, The Times won the 2010 Pulitzer Prize for breaking news, presented for print and online coverage of the assassination of four police officers, and the 2012 Pulitzer Prize for investigative reporting. Boardman is on the Board of Directors of the American Society of News Editors and a past president of Investigative Reporters and Editors. He is a graduate of the Medill School of Journalism at Northwestern University and has a graduate degree from the University of Washington.

"Just Tell Good Stories"

Charles Broadwell, publisher
The Fayetteville Observer
Fayetteville, N.C.

Like a fool, in 1999, when I was the editor, and we were putting in this new press, and we had the U.S. Open golf tournament coming here, and we were planning all this end-of-the-century retrospective with huge, hundred-page sections and all this stuff. I embarked on a series of oral history interviews. I said, "OK. Well, I'll do one." Then it grew. They became 130-inch stories every Sunday in The Observer. It took me back to my roots of why we're here — telling these people's stories. I eventually put the interviews into a book; it became these retrospectives — this slice of history here.

I've covered a lot of bad stuff over the years: crime, accidents, tragedies — horrendous things. But these were things where people you're interviewing brought tears. You — supposedly this hardened journalist — start to tear up a little bit. This was somebody putting his or her life out before the community. To be able to share that for 52 weeks during that year — it was a year like no other for me. I go back to that sometimes when I start to wonder or doubt about the role of the newspaper and all that. Just tell good stories, and I've gotta believe that somebody's going to want those stories, and we'll figure out a way to take care of all this nasty business stuff.

HD video: http://www.whoneedsnewspapers.org/np_interviews.php?npld=epiphany&ivld=epiphany041

Charles Broadwell, the president of Fayetteville Publishing Co., is the 4th generation to lead the family-owned Fayetteville Observer. Broadwell is a Fayetteville native and a Phi Beta Kappa graduate of the University of North Carolina at Chapel Hill. He also has completed fellowship programs at Northwestern University and at the Poynter Institute in St. Petersburg, Fla. Broadwell began his journalism career at age 16 working in The Observer's sports department. He served as the newspaper's editor for more than 10 years and has been the publisher since 2000. Among his professional affiliations, he was president, 2010–11, of the North Carolina Press Association. He serves on the board of the Press Association and the North Carolina Press Foundation (past president). Broadwell is also the author of "Our Century" for the Observer in 1999.

"I Ended Up Engaging People in Our Communities"

Tom Clifford
(Former) Executive News Director
The Post and Courier
Charleston, S.C.

I've done a lot of different kinds of work in newsrooms, but in Florida I had the opportunity to take over a weeklies' operation. I went in and immediately started focusing on the hyper-local service mission and what we were able to do — or not able to do — to serve these communities. I ended up engaging people in our communities at a level and a degree that I had never experienced in any community that I had ever been in. People would call up to talk about their community. They would talk about their neighbor — what their kid did.

We had a kind of dynamic experience happening at the paper where we had to shift focus on these publications, and I turned our weeklies' operation into an operation that focused on the positive achievements of the community's youth. Most of the online was devoted to positive achievements of the community's youth in civic, education, and youth sports — anything that had to do with them. We had huge growth in our website traffic — huge growth in readership based on the reaction I got from readers.

We addressed that age-old complaint — the call from somebody who said, "You never report anything good going on about kids." We were able to say, "Well, actually, in fact, we do. And here's where you can read it in print, and here's where you can see it online." At that time my kids were also in the prime target area, so I was being very selfish about the whole thing. But despite those selfish motivations, I was getting the kind of feedback and reaction that was increasing the reputation of the newspaper in a way that was unique and special and different.

You know there are lots of touchstone moments in people's careers. I did a great investigative report. I brought down a politician. I uncovered graft. I've got those stories. But probably the experience that's most visceral to me was the fact that I was able to take a passion topic for myself — my kids — and apply it to the newspaper in a way that let everybody experience the same thing — through their kids. I never felt closer to the community. I never felt more important to the community. I never felt like I was having as tangible, lasting impact on the community than I did with that project.

HD video: http://www.whoneedsnewspapers.org/np_interviews.php?npld=epiphany &ivld=epiphany044

As director of digital media, **Tom Clifford** was responsible for all digital initiatives, including the presentation of news and advertising on the website, mobile app development, social media and video/multimedia production at The Post and Courier. He started in Charleston in June 2010. Clifford was named executive news director in February 2011. In March 2013, he left The Post and Courier to be executive editor of the Montgomery Advertiser. Clifford previously was editor for digital delivery at Florida Today, overseeing the newspaper's print production and website, as well as managing editor for Custom Publishing, leading the reporting, editing and production of 12 weekly and biweekly publications, and parenting and home-design magazines.

"We'll Tell the Story"

Joe DeLuca, publisher
TampaBay.com (Tampa Bay Times)
St Petersburg, Fla.

Back in 1978, when I was still actually in college and working part-time at a newspaper in Hartford, I was working the evening shift on the copy desk, and it was about one o'clock in the morning, and we would have to take incoming calls. The phone rang — you know you get some interesting calls that time of night into a newsroom — and I picked up the phone, and the caller said that he was across from the Hartford Civic Center and the roof had collapsed.

I immediately figured it was one of those calls that you have to talk your way through, but you can't chase every crazy person that calls at one o'clock in the morning. So I got the person off the phone, and another call came in, and he said that the roof collapsed, and then another and another and another. Every phone in the entire newsroom was ringing with people calling, telling us the roof had collapsed.

At that moment — being a college student — I remember thinking this is an amazing dynamic. I work for a company — a business in this community — and an emergency of that magnitude has occurred, and we're the ones that people want to call, probably right after the police. They want to tell us because they know we'll do something. We'll tell the story. We'll take pictures. We'll chronicle it.

Just watching those phones ring off the hook throughout all the desks in the newsroom, it just struck me that this is a unique place to be. People look at it as an institution — something they want to reach out to in times of trouble. Ever since that day I realized that there's no other kind of company I could work for.

HD video: http://www.whoneedsnewspapers.org/np_interviews.php?npld=epiphany &ivld=epiphany050

Joe DeLuca is a vice president and publisher of both the Tampa edition of the Times and TampaBay.com. He also serves as publisher of tbt*, the company's free daily tabloid. His current leadership portfolio also includes consumer marketing and operations. He serves on the company's executive team and board of directors. DeLuca originally joined The Times in 2001 as director of operations and was named a vice president and director of operations in 2005. Prior to joining The Times, DeLuca was production director of the Hartford (Conn.) Courant, where he also managed the newspaper's commercial printing division, including the printing of Investor's Business Daily for the northeast region. He is a graduate of the University of Hartford with a bachelor's degree in communications.

"You're the Man Who Wrote the Story, Right?"

Nick Ehli, managing editor
The Bozeman Daily Chronicle
Bozeman, Mont.

I was at The Billings Gazette, and my primary beat was crime and justice. I covered a lot of courtrooms and police stations, but I got wind of a story in the small town of Custer, Mont. It's a little farming community outside of Billings about maybe an hour. This little community was trying to start up a football team.

In Montana we have six-man football. There are not enough kids for 11-man football, and so there are schools that play eight-man football and six-man football. The really small schools play six-man football.

In Custer, they had a rancher who donated the edge of a beet field that they were trying to grow grass on. They had a coach who donated all his time, and he just liked football. And they had these kids who wanted to play. It really took this kind of community a Herculean effort to make this happen — letting these six kids come play football on Saturdays. They were there every Saturday. There weren't a lot of people, but they were there — it was bringing together all the small towns.

I got great access to the coach of this team. I let him know I was interested in telling the story, before their first game got played. So I convinced my editor it was a good story. I think he went: "Sports? Really? OK." I snuck out of the newsroom when I could and went down to Custer and spent time with this team. It was really a great narrative with these kids going through this — just all these different people that had come together to make this happen.

The coolest part about that was I went down to watch a game after the story had run. It was all great, in that these kids had gone on and had a good season, and that was just on the side to what the story was really about. But this elderly woman came up and said, "You're the man who wrote the story, right?"

For Custer to be covered in The Billings Gazette was a big deal to begin with. It was this nice story about their community, so I said, "Yeah." But I'm thinking, This could go bad. Did she like the story? Did she not like the story? Her comment was: "I've seen my husband cry on only a couple occasions in his entire life." He was an elderly rancher from Custer. And she goes: "But he cried when he read that story."

And I thought: Well, that was pretty cool.

HD video: http://www.whoneedsnewspapers.org/np_interviews.php?npld=epiphany &ivld=epiphany081

A graduate of the University of Montana School of Journalism, **Nick Ehli** has worked for Montana newspapers as a reporter, editor and columnist for nearly 30 years, including a lengthy stint as a crime reporter for The Billings Gazette. Ehli is the editor-in-chief of *Montana Quarterly* magazine and has edited several regional books. He lives a blissful existence in Bozeman with his wife and two children.

"Journalism with a Big Capital J ... It Touches People"

Gary Farrugia, publisher
The Day
New London, Conn.

I was working at The Philadelphia Inquirer, and I was on the suburban desk on the morning when a plane carrying U.S. Sen. John Heinz collided with a helicopter over a schoolyard — an elementary schoolyard — in suburban Philadelphia. The plane and the helicopter came down. Flaming gasoline was sprayed on the children below. It was horrific.

It happened in an area where a lot of Inquirer reporters lived, and the other thing was — John Heinz was flying to Philadelphia to meet with the editorial board of The Philadelphia Inquirer. So we knew immediately who was on that plane.

Because so many people who worked at the paper lived in the area, we had access to the neighbors. We had access to the parents of the children who were at the school. As luck would have it, I had a reporter in that school at that moment when the accident happened. He watched an 8-year-old boy on fire, coming into the school. A 58-year-old woman, Ivy Weeks, who was a volunteer reader, took that boy and embraced him in her bosom and literally snuffed the flames out of the boy — David Rutenberg — and the boy lived.

My reporter watched that happen. So we were able to tell this story in the large sense of what a catastrophic thing this was — to lose a United States Senator. But it became a very human story about dignity and heroism. That story just resonated for weeks and weeks and weeks.

Two years later we were sitting at a focus group because we were about to launch a new zoning thing — The Inquirer was making all this noise about zoning. The focus group director asked one of the participants about how the paper affected him, and we were standing behind the glass screen, and we watched this. This man described this story that I just told you about. He described the page where certain graphic information was. He said on page 6-A they had a list of everybody who died in that, and nobody had that before.

It was at that moment I realized that when you have journalism with a big capital J, that it touches people in ways you can't even comprehend sometimes.

HD video: http://www.whoneedsnewspapers.org/np_interviews.php?npld=epiphany&ivld=epiphany019

Gary Farrugia became publisher of The Day Publishing Co. in January 2002. Before arriving in New London, Farrugia worked 18 years at The Philadelphia Inquirer. In 1991, he led a reporting team that was a Pulitzer Prize finalist for coverage of the death of U.S. Sen. John Heinz and seven others in a mid-air collision above a crowded Philadelphia schoolyard. In 1994, Farrugia became news director of "Inquirer News Tonight," a nightly newscast that aired on a local Philadelphia broadcast television station. In 1996, Farrugia returned to the newspaper to head KR Video, a television documentary production company. KR Video produced documentaries for CNN and PBS including *Black Hawk Down*, which became a best-selling book and major motion picture. In 2000, Farrugia was named vice president for new business development at The Inquirer. There, he managed five subsidiary companies including KR Video, Database Marketing, Broad Street Custom Publishing, News Research and PhillyTech Magazine.

"We're Going to Print and Deliver Our Papers"

Clay Foster, CEO and publisher
The Northeast Mississippi Daily Journal
Tupelo, Miss.

We had a snowstorm hit here the first full week of January, a few weeks ago, and snow really cripples Mississippi. We're just not used to snow. We struggled getting people into work that day. But, obviously, we start every day with the expectation we're going to print and deliver our papers — someway, somehow.

We were very short staffed, so I was one of three people who were manning the phones that day. Our phones were ringing off the hook. Over the course of two days until the snow cleared enough for us to get back to 100 percent delivery, we received over 1,500 calls from our customers. Most were OK with it, but wondering where their paper was, and wondering when we were going to get there.

You know, you've got people looking out their window who are scared to walk outside because of the snow and ice, but they're wondering why you didn't get the paper to them. That sends a very powerful message. So, when someone asks me about the future of print — and I'm on the phone listening to 1,500-plus customers over a two-or-three-day period — I'm thinking: Wow! We've got a tremendous opportunity, going forward.

The print newspaper is very important to a significant part of the folks that live in this community. They've grown up with it, or they've come, over time, to it. It's become a very integral part of their life. They just miss it when it's not there.

HD video: http://www.whoneedsnewspapers.org/np_interviews.php?npld=epiphany &ivld=epiphany054

Clay Foster is a native son of Northeast Mississippi. In addition to being a carrier early in his life and until he graduated from the University of Mississippi, Foster has been with The Journal in a full-time capacity since 1992 and has been chief operating officer since 2000. He assumed the additional titles of president in 2005 and publisher in 2010. His career at The Journal has included stints as pre-press manager, production director and director of operations, as well as interim assignments as advertising director and circulation director. He is also a retired major in the Mississippi Army National Guard, having served 22 years, including 15 months in Operation Iraqi Freedom.

"A Better Understanding of the Issues Facing Our Community"

John B. Johnson
(Former) V.P. and General Manager
Johnson Newspaper Corp./The Watertown
Daily Times
Watertown, N.Y.

I think it matters when you go to a small diner in Alexandria Bay (N.Y.) for breakfast on a Sunday morning, and sitting at the counter are three people — each reading a copy of the Sunday newspaper — having an argument about what's going to happen down the river in Cape Vincent because of some decisions that were made by the board of supervisors around wind towers and wind setbacks. To see three friends talking and arguing about it means that those three guys or those three women are going to walk away with a better understanding of the issues that are facing the community.

Personally, I love the great turn of phrase. I love great writing. I can move through something like The Wall Street Journal and read some of the fabulous opinion pieces — especially over the past two years as the country has gone through some interesting changes. And I come away feeling just more aware of what's going on, and it's good, right?

You know this life is short. You can't put another quarter in when you reach the end. Your life becomes richer the more interaction you have with people. And it's better, I think, to have interaction with people on some issues of substance that make a difference for the next generation that's coming. I think that is really important. I feel like I get that from reading. I feel like I get that from some of the journalism.

I feel like I get a lot of evil glares, too, from people about the journalism — and I think that's good, too. You've got to have a thick skin in this business.

HD video: http://www.whoneedsnewspapers.org/np_interviews.php?npld=epiphany &ivld=epiphany007

Following graduation from Wesleyan University in 1994, **John Johnson** moved to Chicago to work for Rand McNally and Company as a children's book editor and as a marketing manager for Rand McNally's TripMaker software. After four years at Rand McNally, Johnson earned an MBA from the Kellogg School of Management at Northwestern University in 2002, after which he and his wife Kate moved to Minneapolis/St. Paul where Johnson took a job with 3M. At 3M, he was the group business unit manager responsible for a portfolio of business teams within the Post-it brand. Johnson returned to Watertown in August of 2008 to join the Johnson Newspaper Corporation where he is the vice president and general manager of Northern New York Newspaper Corp., the largest division in the Johnson Newspaper Corp. In that role, he has operating and strategic responsibility for a portfolio of daily and weekly publications and their associated websites. In May 2013, Johnson was named CEO at Johnson Newspaper Corp.

"These Young People Put Their Lives on the Line to Keep People Informed"

Keith Magill, executive editor
The Courier
Houma, La.

Katrina was monumental. I'm born and raised in New Orleans, and I have family and friends there and some who had really, really rough times. Some who were lucky to make it through with minimal damages to their homes and people that they love.

We thought we're going to get a direct hit here, but it jogged just east right before it hit the coast. It looked like it was going to be a category-four storm.

Most every storm that I can remember, the newsroom will get together, and I'll say, "Look, I'm not going to force anybody to stay in harm's way. And I mean it. If you feel it's not the right thing for you to do, I want you to just be able to go, and with no repercussions and with no concern other than your safety." And most people, in Katrina, said, "I would prefer to go." But we had two people stay in the courthouse with police, [and] fire-[fighters] — first-responder-type folks. They sent news dispatches through a laptop to a Palm Pilot in our car as we drove away, because we left just long enough for the storm to pass.

We posted things onto the web constantly from a Palm Pilot in the car on the way to one of our staff member's parents' houses in Monroe. We never stopped working and publishing stories online the whole time, even if we weren't sitting here in the newsroom.

The willingness of these young journalists to put their lives on the line to keep people informed about what was happening to them under the most uncertain and difficult times — that impressed me. It impressed upon me what we really have here as a group of people. That kind of dedication is hard to find in any field, in any walk of life, but to see it in my own newsroom — it just made me realize what we really have — how powerful a mission it is, and how seriously the people who do it, take it.

HD video: http://www.whoneedsnewspapers.org/np_interviews.php?npld=epiphany &ivld=epiphany057

Keith Magill is executive editor of The Courier in Houma, La., and its sister paper, The Daily Comet in Thibodaux, La. He has spent most of his 26-year career at the papers, with stints as a reporter at The Wilmington Star-News in North Carolina and as city editor at The Tuscaloosa (Ala.) News. The Louisiana Press Association named The Courier, under Magill's leadership, Newspaper of the Year in its circulation category for the past six years. Magill, an award-winning columnist, was recognized statewide and regionally for his authoritative essays about two of his community's most pressing issues: hurricane protection and coastal land loss. He graduated from Loyola University in his hometown, New Orleans.

"These Are Our People. How Do We Best Serve Them?"

Meg Martin
(Former) Online Editor
The Roanoke Times
Roanoke, Va.

My first real day in the newsroom was April 16, 2007. I had been here for two weeks. It was my first day with the training wheels off, figuring out what it was going to be like in The Roanoke Times newsroom. It was a normal day until about 9 o'clock in the morning, and that was when we found out about the shootings at Virginia Tech, and everything changed. Everything changed for a very, very long time — and maybe forever.

I was obviously very new to the newsroom, and my contribution was basically — do whatever they need you to do, and do whatever you know how to do, and don't get in anyone's way.

I learned a lot in the first couple of hours about the place where I had landed and about the people and the news organization I was working for. I kept hearing — in so many words — about all the decisions people were making. Some simple things like when to publish names and who to contact and who to talk to.

I kept hearing the same conversation over and over again — people saying: "This is our community. These are our people. How do we best serve them?" It wasn't put on. It wasn't fake. It wasn't: Oh, I guess we should probably have this conversation. It was real, and it was genuine.

I remember I wrote to my mom late, late that night — because I'd been in the newsroom for like 20 hours — telling her that I knew I had come to the right place even under these awful circumstances because people were asking these questions that I didn't think people actually asked. That I had read about in my textbooks that I didn't think people actually asked in real newsrooms — but they were.

I was hearing these conversations asked by the editor and by the metro editors and reporters, saying, "How are we going to best serve our community and how are we going to make sure that — tomorrow and next week and next month — that when we run into people in the community, in the grocery store, that we're going to be proud of the work we've done? And they're going to be able to know that we're serving them in the right way." That's when I knew I had come to the right place. I was really proud to have been able to work with people like that.

HD video: http://www.whoneedsnewspapers.org/np_interviews.php?npld=epiphany &ivld=epiphany040

Meg Martin joined the online team of The Roanoke Times as a multimedia producer in 2007, after spending two years at The Poynter Institute — first as a summer writing fellow and later as a fellow and editor at Poynter Online. A Pittsburgh native, Martin graduated from the University of Notre Dame in 2005 with a degree in English and a focus on oral storytelling and family narrative. She's a member of the Online News Association, the Society for News Design and the Appalachian Studies Association. Martin joined American Public Media as associate editor, Public Insight Network, in May 2012.

"It Was Our First Special Edition Since Pearl Harbor"

Debra C. Meade, president and publisher
The Roanoke Times
Roanoke, Va.

It was on 9/11, and I was the circulation director then. That morning we'd been in an executive meeting — the publisher and her executive team were offsite. And we got word that a plane had flown into the World Trade Center. At first we thought — like everyone — it was an errant plane or a private plane. Then we got an idea of how terrible and huge this disaster was. So we came back here immediately and reconvened, and we put out a special edition of The Roanoke Times. It was our first special edition of the paper since Pearl Harbor.

I wasn't here for Pearl Harbor, but I've heard about that one, and we still have copies of it in our archives. It was a smaller eight-page section with what was known at the time, and it rolled off the presses.

I actually hawked the [9/11] paper that evening — all evening — on the street corner in front of our building. We decided to give the paper away — as a public service. Also because it would have been so terribly difficult to try to get money for it, we couldn't have made change. We just wanted to distribute the news and fulfill that mission the easiest and best way we could think of under such extraordinary circumstances.

People were driving up in cars, and we were just sort of flinging the newspaper into passing vehicles. It's a miracle we didn't have an accident out there because the streets were clogged. And so many people just said, "Thank you. Thank you, so much for doing this for us." So I had my news bag and papers and reloaded and did that all [evening]. At the end of that day I remember thinking, "Gosh, this is one of those days when you really feel like you've fulfilled the mission."

HD video: http://www.whoneedsnewspapers.org/np_interviews.php?npId=epiphany &ivId=epiphany038

With a career that spans more than two decades at The Roanoke Times, **Debbie Meade** has a broad functional background in the newspaper business, as well as leadership experience across departments. Before becoming publisher in February 2007, she served as The Times' advertising director, circulation director, retail advertising manager, human resources director, circulation marketing manager, assistant to the president and publisher, and assistant bureau chief. A Norfolk, Va., native, Meade also spent her childhood in Richmond, Va., and the small town of Lebanon, Va. She holds a bachelor's and a master's degree from Virginia Tech.

"We Have Opportunities in Our Business to Help Others"

Otis Raybon Jr., (former) publisher
The Rome News-Tribune
Rome, Ga.

I guess when I really saw what we could do — the power of newspapers — was in Americus, Ga., when a good friend of my family (a veterinarian) came by my office one day. He had just built a new house, and he says, "I'm going to sell my house." I said, "Sam, you're crazy. Why?" And he said he and his wife felt the call to go to the missionary field. And they did.

In 1996, my wife and I and my two sons visited them in Trujillo, Peru. We spent almost 10 days there. He [our friend] had a need for New Testaments that he could take with him when he visited in the remote mountainous areas of Peru — for the tribes. He wanted to leave a New Testament behind.

I came back from that trip, and I wrote a story about our experience in Peru, with Sam and his wife, Janet, and their children. And, as a little side note, I wrote that Sam had a need for New Testaments. He needed about $3,500–$5,000.

Because of the story, we raised that money. We were able to send him about $3,500 and helped him acquire those Bibles and helped him leave those Bibles behind as he made his travels.

I knew how important our newspaper was, but I guess that was the most personal thing that solidified for me that we have an opportunity in our business to help others in varying degrees. It may not be a trip to visit a missionary friend — it could be anything — but we have opportunities in this business to help others and to help our communities.

HD video: http://www.whoneedsnewspapers.org/np_interviews.php?npId=epiphany &ivId=epiphany045

Otis Raybon Jr. retired from The Rome News-Tribune in August 2013. Raybon came to The Rome News-Tribune in 1998 as V.P. operations, News Publishing Company, The Rome News-Tribune's parent company. In 2008, Raybon was named publisher of The News-Tribune along with responsibility for six weekly newspapers in NW Georgia and Alabama — including direct mail, magazine coupon booklets, and senior citizen publications. Previously, he was publisher of The Dalton Daily Citizen News, The Griffin Daily News and The Americus Times Recorder. Raybon has served on the board of the Georgia Press Association. He has a degree in marketing from Georgia State University.

"Leave Your Community Better than When You Found It"

Dolph C. Simons Jr.
Chairman, The World Co.
Editor & Publisher, The Lawrence Journal-World
Lawrence, Kan.

I was out at my grandfather's house on Dec. 7, 1941 — Sunday. We always had dinner with my grandparents. I was lying on the floor, and I heard about Pearl Harbor, and Dad said, "We're gonna put out an extra." So we put out an extra on that Sunday. We had no Sunday paper.

My brother and I were given whistles — like a referee's whistle — and we were walking up and down the streets blowing our whistle yelling, "Extra, extra!" Whether it was blowin' the whistle on "Extra, extra!" — I was 11 years old then, and my brother was 9 — selling extras was a thing that got me involved.

I always seemed to want to be in the newspaper business. I just can't imagine any other business that would be more interesting, fun, and you want to leave your community better than when you found it, but I think a paper — or whatever we're going to call a paper — can indeed do that.

I'm frustrated; I tell you can just sense it. People ought to be busting their guts trying to figure out how to keep newspapers alive. If we could project ourselves out 10 years from now, and then look back and say, "Why didn't we grab that opportunity? It was there, and we didn't have the smarts or the courage to go ahead and do it?"

I'll be dead one of these days pretty quick, but I would like to figure out how in the hell do we come up with a plan to take advantage of the opportunities to keep newspapers alive. I think we have this responsibility — to try to inform the public.

HD video: http://www.whoneedsnewspapers.org/np_interviews.php?npId=epiphany &ivId=epiphany089

Dolph Simons Jr. has been a director of the Associated Press; president of the Kansas Associated Press board of directors; director of the Inland Daily Press Association; director and president of the Kansas Press Association; trustee and board president of the William Allen White Foundation, which works to promote the journalistic ideals of the former Emporia, Kan., newspaper editor; and a Pulitzer Prize juror. He served as a director and board secretary of the American Newspaper Publishers Association (now Newspaper Association of America). He also is a former director of the Newspaper Advertising Bureau, Inc. Under his leadership, the World Company, headquartered in Lawrence, Kan., was until October 2010 one of the most integrated multimedia companies in the nation. At that time, the company sold its broadband division and is now focused on print and digital communication activities.

"Communicating About Our Community — That's What We Do"

Ginny Sohn, publisher
The Santa Fe New Mexican
Santa Fe, N.M.

I attended a town hall meeting with two of our local politicians — a senator and a congressman. The town hall meeting was packed, and there was some conversation from someone who recently moved to Santa Fe, N.M., from California. He did quite a bit of bashing of the state of New Mexico and found fault in a lot of areas. So, a local man — of Spanish descent — whose family had been here for generations, stood up and began speaking.

And recently The New Mexican had published a small magazine called *The 400 and Beyond*. It was written by local high school students about our 400th anniversary. One of the very good essays written in this publication was written by our local senator's son — who is an Anglo. He wrote about the culture and the diversity of Santa Fe, and what it meant to him to live here and be raised here and go to school here.

This man of Spanish descent stood up in the town hall meeting and said to the senator, "I read the piece that was written by your son. And I just want to thank you because many people do not understand and don't really get what it is we have here that is such a jewel — the diversity of the land of enchantment of Santa Fe." He [the senator] thanked him, and said, "Oh, we're such a crappy town — that's why all these people from California want to come and live here."

So just getting that across and bringing together and communicating the information, and the problems and the good things about our community — that's what we do.

HD video: http://www.whoneedsnewspapers.org/np_interviews.php?npld=epiphany&ivld=epiphany061

Ginny Sohn was named publisher of The Santa Fe New Mexican in April 2012 after serving as associate publisher for five years. Prior to that, she was the advertising director. She began her career in publishing in 1974 in New York City working for Conde Nast Publications. After relocating to Santa Fe, N.M., she began working for The New Mexican while it was a Gannett paper and in the mid-1980s was promoted to ad director at The Reno Gazette Journal. In 1989 she returned to The New Mexican as ad director and later that year the paper once again was back to independent ownership. Sohn holds a bachelor of science in business administration and management from the University of Phoenix. She and her son, Sage, live in Santa Fe.

"It Still Gives Me Chills"

Kirsten Stromsodt
(Former) Assigning Editor
The Grand Forks Herald
Grand Forks, N.D.

I was very young, but I didn't realize then where I wanted to go in the field of journalism. I didn't know if I wanted to be on TV or if I wanted to work at a newspaper, and then the flood of '97 happened.

I was a senior in high school; I went to a small school in rural Grand Forks County. I grew up reading the newspaper. I remember one of my first memories was pretending to read the comics to my dad when I was about 4.

Anyway, during the flood, our school was canceled, and the paper had difficulty printing. What The Herald was doing was distributing a paper every day at about five or six to different drop-off locations around the city.

I was sent to Emerado (N.D.) — a town just right by the (Grand Forks) Air Force Base, which is five miles from where we lived — to get the free paper. I remember going to that gas station and watching people crowded around that truck as they were throwing off bundles of Heralds. It still gives me chills, to this day, to see how important that [newspaper] was to those people. I was done. It solidified my calling.

I graduated, and that fall I went into The Herald, and I walked in and said, I want to work here. I worked here through college, and then they just felt like keeping me around.

In 2007, something reminded me of that experience. The small town of Northwood (N.D.) was leveled by a tornado, and I happened to be in that Sunday night doing some catch-up work, and all of a sudden the tornado hits, and it's just mass chaos. I went home at about five in the morning and slept for two hours and came back in, and we put out a special section and distributed it free.

We serve a purpose. People feel we're important. I put out three papers in 24 hours that day. I was on the copy desk then. It was something else.

HD video: http://www.whoneedsnewspapers.org/np_interviews.php?npld=epiphany &ivld=epiphany101

Kirsten Stromsodt started at The Herald in the fall of 1998, working as a part-time sports clerk. After graduating from the University of North Dakota, in 2001, she was hired full-time on the news copy desk. Subsequently, she was promoted to news editor, night editor and assigning editor in 2009. Stromsodt is a native of rural Grand Forks County. She is currently deputy editor of The Forum of Fargo-Moorehead.

"We Focused on the Victims"

Carole Tarrant, (former) editor
The Roanoke Times
Roanoke, Va.

A clarifying moment for me has been working here during the shootings at Virginia Tech. I think I really understood what a newspaper could do in the community at that point. We were very much that connective fiber that people were looking to for answers that we could help provide them. The website performed a great role in getting more information out much more quickly — the pace of the print edition was just a dinosaur. It was way too slow for what was happening right then. So our role was getting information out, but fact-checking it and being a calming presence.

In those first few days and in those first few hours, it was just chaos — people were really looking to us for help to understand this and make sense of that. And we could do that. The thank-yous that we got for that were passionate about the role that we played. It was the calming — because we saw such a difference in the national media.

The national media was: Who did what, and why, and who can we blame? It was stirring the pot, which I can understand from a national perspective, but as a community paper we really needed to be in tune with what the community mood was then, and what they needed — to share the mourning.

We focused at that point on the victims because we thought everybody deserved a very good story of who they were. We just turned the whole newsroom over to that, versus launching into: Who did what and who's to blame? I know that stuff comes out. I knew there would be a special blue-ribbon task force, and there'd be plenty of time for that.

But in the immediacy — right after the shooting — it was: Who had died, and how could we remember them?

HD video: http://www.whoneedsnewspapers.org/np_interviews.php?npld=epiphany &ivld=epiphany039

Carole Tarrant joined The Roanoke Times in 2005 and became editor in 2007. During her tenure, the paper and its website, roanoke.com, have won a number of national awards for photojournalism, breaking news, enterprise and multimedia reporting. The Scripps Howard Foundation, Pictures of the Year International, *Editor & Publisher* magazine and the Online News Association are among the organizations recognizing this work. Tarrant has served on the national board of the Associated Press Managing Editors and is a member of the Journalism and Women Symposium (JAWS). A Philadelphia native, she previously worked at newspapers in North Dakota, Florida and Alabama. She lives in Salem, Va., with her son. Tarrant left The Times in October 2013 and is now at Virginia Western Community College in Roanoke.

"It Was the Information That People Needed to Know"

John Walker, website coordinator
The Opelika-Auburn News
Opelika, Ala.

My first year working in radio at my college, the advantage to our station was — it was an actual commercial radio station with a 60-mile range.

I remember within my first month or two working there, we had one day of tornadoes that were just popping up left and right in Mississippi, and a lot of people lost power during this.

I thought: How are people going to find out about this kind of stuff if they don't have power? Then I remembered the simplest thing — battery-powered radios.

People were able to tune into our radio station and find out where the tornadoes were. Where the damage was. What to avoid. Where to go. It was the need to know what to do. The need to know what's going on in your community. It's people wanting to know what's going on.

So I figured: I like doing this. I like being that voice of information for people. I guess that's what really clicked for me. It was tornadoes. It was information that people needed to know on the spot, right then and there — let's give it to them. Let's not wait. Let's do it now. Let's help the public. Let's get them the information they need.

HD video: http://www.whoneedsnewspapers.org/np_interviews.php?npld=epiphany &ivld=epiphany053

John Walker began at Media General in 2005 as the online producer for WJTV News Channel 12 in Jackson, Miss., before relocating to Opelika, Ala., in March 2008. He is currently the website coordinator for OANow.com and WRBL.com. Walker oversees online multimedia content for the sites and works with other news properties in sharing content. He has run production of various weekly video projects involving talent from the newspaper including sports, news, and community.

Section IV

CHALLENGING
AUTHORITY

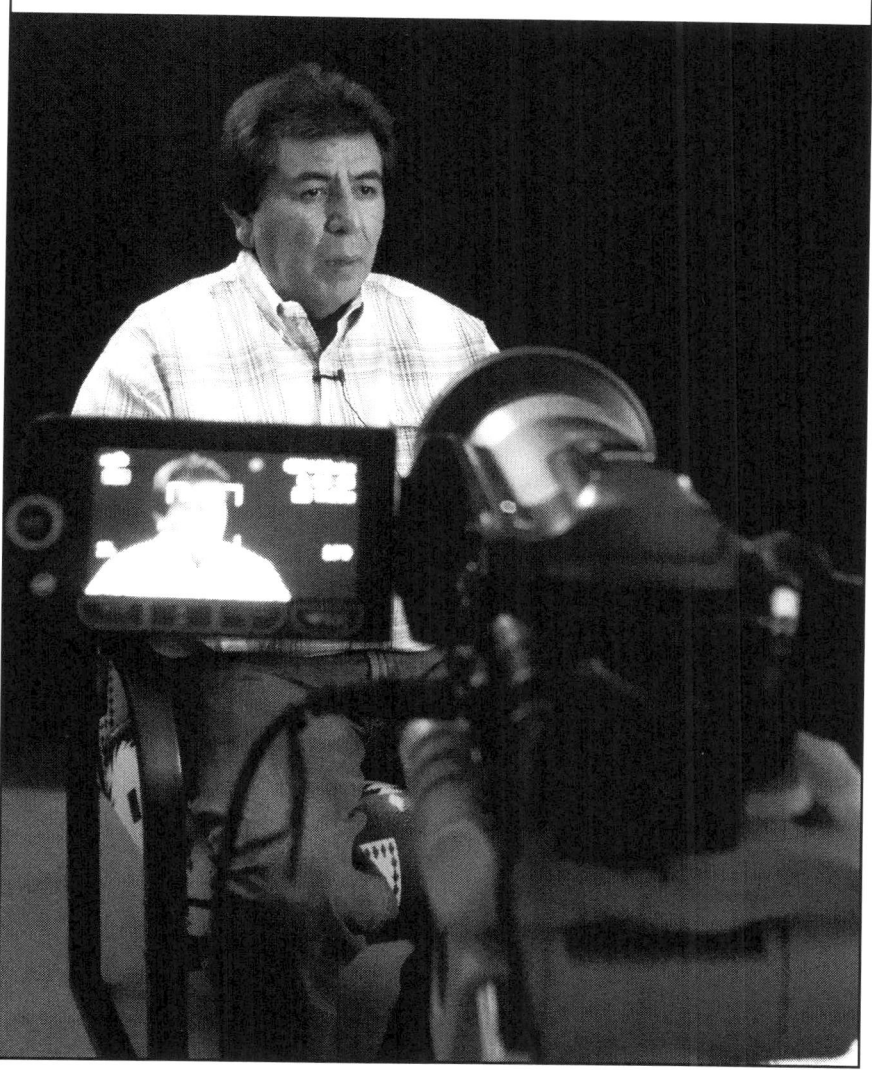

Challenging Authority

Confronting authority can be a lonely enterprise, but — unless you are a student journalist writing for your school's newspaper — it is usually shielded by the power of the press. Student journalists, writing for newspapers in high schools and colleges, may discover the risks of confronting power early in their careers. They're too often called on the carpet if their stories or editorials conflict with the agenda of a high school principal, a school board or a college president.

Community newspaper publishers discover their publication's clout when it conflicts with the aims of important local businesses or elected officials. News stories that threaten the local establishment can trigger threats of economic punishment or litigation.

When confronting authority, reporters need to learn the simple lesson that Nathan Eagle, former managing editor of The Garden Island, discovered early in his career: "You've got to be strong enough to stand up behind the story."

In this section, professional journalists share personal epiphanies about how challenging authority threatened their livelihood, how they managed these threats and what happened when they did.

"There's a Reason Why I'm Here"

Tom Arviso Jr., publisher
The Navajo Times
Window Rock, Ariz.

When our [Tribal] President Albert Hale came into office, things started to unravel about some extramarital affair going on in his office and some misuse of a credit card — things we weren't really benefiting from — at least nothing that we could see. So we reported on those things.

It was a time when our role with the native press was questioned by our government. They said, "Why are you writing all these things about our leader when in fact it's not true?" We said, "We're writing about stuff that's based on fact. Look at the financial records. Look at the pictures we have." We had factual information to back this up, but we were really questioning our role.

We had a story we were going to break about the extramarital affair and the credit card, and that afternoon I got called into our president's office. We had a man-to-man talk. No tape recorders. We had an agreement that we wouldn't talk about what we discussed. That was with Mr. Hale.

I left there from his office thinking: What am I going to do? Cause Albert was a good friend of mine, too. We used to play basketball long ago, and I got to know him, and the lady he was involved with was a former classmate of mine. So they were former friends — people I knew. But I also knew the office that they held and the public trust that people put into what they were doing.

So I came back, and I thought: What are we going to do? Are we going to break this story? Or am I going to hold off on it until I get more information? I came to realize we had enough to break the story. So we did. It came out the next morning — a huge story. And everything took off from there. After that, eventually, he had to resign from office or he was going to face prosecution. I wish it could've been something different.

From a personal standpoint, it was really stressful. I went through a lot of asking myself: Why am I doing this? Why me? I came to realize: Hey, there's a reason why I am here. There's a reason why I'm in this position. There's a reason why I've got to make this decision.

So I stuck with it. We ran the story, and things just took care of themselves. Truth always prevails.

HD video: http://www.whoneedsnewspapers.org/np_interviews.php?npId=epiphany &ivId=epiphany065

Tom Arviso Jr. majored in journalism at Arizona State University. He became managing editor of The Navajo Times in October 1988, editor and publisher in 1993, and was named CEO of the Navajo Times Publishing Company in 2004. Arviso is a former board vice president and treasurer of the Native American Journalists Association's Board of Directors, a member of the Arizona Newspapers Association's Board of Directors and a board member of UNITY — Journalists of Color. He has received the John Peter and Anna Catherine Zenger Award for Freedom of the Press and the People's Right to Know, a John S. Knight Fellowship in Journalism, 2000–2001, at Stanford University, the Arizona Newspapers Association Freedom of Information Award and The Native American Journalists Association's Wassaja Award, for extraordinary service to Native journalism.

"That Piece of Journalism Had an Immediate Impact"

Martin Baron, (former) editor
The Boston Globe
Boston, Mass.

There are many instances as an editor of where you see the importance of journalism.

Shortly after I came here to The Globe, we launched an investigation of sexual abuse by priests within the Roman Catholic Church. And more important than just the fact of sexual abuse was the issue of whether there had been a decades-long cover-up of priests who had engaged in sexual abuse of young children.

In fact, we documented that there had been a cover-up. It had lasted 40 years or more, and that piece of journalism has had an immediate impact.

It's had an enduring impact — not just on this community, but on the entire country — particularly the practices of the Roman Catholic Church. And now, throughout the world.

I think it was a tremendously important piece of journalism. And its effects are going to be felt for many decades to come.

HD video: http://www.whoneedsnewspapers.org/np_interviews.php?npld=epiphany &ivld=epiphany017

Martin Baron was named executive editor of The Washington Post in 2013. Prior to joining The Post, Baron was editor of The Boston Globe, in 2001, and was executive editor of The Miami Herald, when the paper won a Pulitzer Prize for breaking news coverage. Baron began his career as a state reporter and then business writer at The Miami Herald. He moved to The Los Angeles Times as a reporter in 1979, later becoming business editor and assistant managing editor. He rejoined The Miami Herald in 1996 and became executive editor at The Miami Herald in 2000. Baron graduated from Lehigh University with BA and MBA degrees.

"There Was Pressure to Back Off"

Frank Blethen, publisher
The Seattle Times
Seattle, Wash.

There are two moments I'm particularly proud of. One is the Pulitzer-Prize-winning piece that we did investigating the [Boeing] 737 and the problem with its tail, which was a safety issue. There was a lot of pressure put on us to back off that story. In fact, there was even a tremendous amount of pressure put on the Pulitzer Board not to give us a Pulitzer for that story.

About a year after the story, I got a phone call out of the blue from a woman who identified herself as one of the founders of — I forget what the group is called — but it's airline employees and pilots that have been killed in a 737 crash. She said, "I was talking to your reporter the other day, and I asked him who's responsible for you guys pursuing this, and he said the Blethen family." She said, "Can I thank them?"

She ends up telling me what a difference this made and talked about the lives we've saved and what a difference it made to the survivors. That was pretty powerful.

The other one was when U.S. Rep. Brock Adams had turned into a sexual predator and was preying on his staff. [Times investigative reporter and, subsequently, Executive Editor] Dave Boardman came up with this incredibly innovative solution, which was to get affidavits from the victims that they would testify in court if Adams brought an action against us. I believe we had 15 names, and I think 11 or 12 of them actually signed these affidavits. So it made it a no-brainer. It was actually the only time I ever know of when a newspaper could use confidential sources and yet have a credible story and a defensible story.

In fact, our editor at the time, Mike Fancher, came in and said, "You need to know how serious this is. The Adams' people and the Democrats say they're going to take this newspaper away from you if you run the story. That's their claim."

When he laid it out for me, I said, "Hell, this is an easy decision. You know there's no way Adams is ever going to take the stand when he knows these women will take the stand." That's precisely what happened, and then [Adams] resigned.

I think both of those are symbolic of things that we've done as an independent newspaper in terms of being able to independently tell these important stories, especially around public safety, around women and children.

HD video: http://www.whoneedsnewspapers.org/np_interviews.php?npld=epiphany &ivld=epiphany075

Frank Blethen, publisher of The Seattle Times, is a member of the fourth generation of family newspaper ownership. There are ten members of the family's fourth and fifth generations active in the journalism company's management and governance. Blethen is a strong advocate for independent journalism, family-owned businesses, and a longtime active participant in the national grassroots movement in opposition to newspaper and media ownership consolidation. In recognition of Blethen's leadership on behalf of quality journalism, he was the first publisher awarded the American Society of News Editors' News Leadership Award.

"If You ... Stick to Your Guns ..., the Right Things Can Happen"

Laurena Mayne Davis, managing editor
The Daily Sentinel
Grand Junction, Colo.

I was an advisor at a student newspaper, and student media have even more of a challenge. They're more at a power differential in their careers.

There was an editor who discovered that there were some things that should have happened in open meetings with the board of trustees that clearly didn't happen — weren't talked about — and yet a decision was made. That editor went after those recorded minutes from executive session to try to find out if the discussion happened. The discussion was about a job description for president — a new president for the college.

That was an uphill battle for her. It ended up in the courts. She had to go on her own because she was an employee of the college as well, so she did this personally, outside her role as editor, and she faced a lot of criticism — a lot of pushback — from the campus community.

She stuck it out; she got the information.

I'm proud to say now she's received her doctorate in journalism, and not just because of that event. She was a strong student before who had a lot of good teachers who had influenced her.

What that event did for her and for me — as student advisor — was to realize that if you do things for the right reasons and stick to your guns, even from a student-to-administration level on a college campus, the right things can happen. The right information can come out.

HD video: http://www.whoneedsnewspapers.org/np_interviews.php?npld=epiphany &ivld=epiphany086

Managing Editor **Laurena Mayne Davis** started at The Sentinel in 1992 as a college intern and was a copy editor, reporter and features editor before becoming managing editor in 2008. Previously she taught journalism at Northern Arizona University and Mesa State College. Davis has been a fellow at the American Press Institute and the Poynter Institute and has written two books and edited two others, including the *2011 Monumental Majesty: 100 Years of Colorado National Monument.*

"The Power of Journalism Could Get Some Quick Change"

Nathan Eagle
(Former) Managing Editor
The Garden Island
Lihue, Kauai, Hawaii

In high school, my senior year, I got talked into writing for the newspaper, and an issue popped up. I was a student athlete and one of my friends was allowed to play more than one varsity sport per season, which I had been excited to do — soccer and cross-country. But I was told I couldn't because it was one sport per season. So I wrote a story about that for our school newspaper, and the next day I found myself in the AD's office being asked why did you do this and why did you do that?

I learned a lot in that instance. I learned the power of journalism could get some quick change. They went back and changed the code. I don't think that they had ever been questioned before.

Another example was taking on a very prominent deacon of the church and businessman at the first daily paper I worked for. He, on the side, ran a trailer park, which literally had sewage running right down the road. I called him and I said, "Hey, what's going on here?"

He said," I don't know what you're talking about."

I showed up, and I showed him photos, and I interviewed the residents and got their stories about how they'd been impacted by this.

I think he was trying to call my bluff — the deacon — and he said, "No, you are not going to write this because of who I am. Because of who you are. And look at who they are." But we ran it.

I had a great editor at the time who helped me make sure all my facts were checked and my i's were dotted and t's were crossed.

Sure enough, the EPA was out soon thereafter; there were fines issued. The trailer park was cleaned up, and suddenly, right after that clean up, he closed it.

I sure learned the impact that a good story can have. I also learned there is a backlash that you have to be able to stand up to and take. That was my first time experiencing that.

He would go on to the city council in public forums and utilize his TV time to bash me and the paper for ruining his life.

So that first got me second-guessing the story: Did I do something wrong? Then, ultimately, I learned that you've got to be strong enough to stand up behind the story.

HD video: http://www.whoneedsnewspapers.org/np_interviews.php?npId=epiphany &ivId=epiphany070

In 2011, **Nathan Eagle** lived, worked and played on Kauai. An Ohio native, his passion for exploring new cultures had taken him from Spain to the middle of the Pacific. Starting as an environmental reporter, he served as managing editor of The Garden Island. Eagle's passion remained fixed on holding elected officials accountable, providing a voice for endangered species and serving the community by delivering timely, accurate stories on the issues that matter most. Preserving journalistic integrity and maintaining high ethics were the foundation of his daily decisions. When Eagle was not in the office doing his best to build his team of dedicated reporters — and improving his own performance through constant self-criticism — he was either in the water free diving or on the side of a mountain hiking.

"It Impacted People's Lives"

Kurt Johnson, copublisher
The Aurora News-Register
Aurora, Neb.

I've had a lot of experiences where I've felt like we have impacted individual families or people's lives with a particular feature story or something, but when I was executive editor of a daily in South Dakota, the university in town was owned by a Japanese gentleman. He wanted to show his Japanese counterparts that he owned an American university, and he was kind of used to running his own show and calling his own shots.

So in the process of reporting, my first cousin was in Tokyo, and I developed an email relationship with a friend of his who was working at this university. I began to get information about enrollment straight from the registrar's office that was completely different than what I was hearing from the Japanese owner when he came to South Dakota to talk about it.

I had to be very careful how I used that source, but I was asking questions and actually showing him some documents, and at first he was very offended, and he said, "Where did you get this?" He began to answer my questions, and — long story short — over a course of about two years, he lost his accreditation.

Right before he was going to lose his accreditation, he was forced to sell, and I'm just absolutely convinced the newspaper's coverage of that exposed what was really going on before a lot of people knew about it. He was beefing up his numbers as far as Japanese enrollment — students that were being sent — and where the finances were. It was just not an accurate picture.

So in the town of 14,000, a university — or not having a university — was a huge, huge deal then as it is today.

So it struck me then — I was feeling the heat of it, getting visits from the on-site campus president asking me where was I getting this information — that this wasn't just an ironic, cute game. It was a big deal. It impacted people's lives and the whole community.

That was really an eye-opener for me. This is serious business, and you need to treat it that way.

HD video: http://www.whoneedsnewspapers.org/np_interviews.php?npId=epiphany&ivId=epiphany091

The Aurora News-Register Co-Publisher **Kurt Johnson** grew up in a newspaper family. His parents, Elna and Loral Johnson, established Johnson Publications, Inc., with papers in Imperial, Wauneta, and Grant, Neb., and just across the border in Holyoke, Colo. After earning a journalism/business degree from Kearney State College in 1985, Johnson worked in news-editorial management with newspapers in five states, before he and his wife, Paula, purchased The Aurora News-Register in 2000.

"We Persevered, Pressed through, Published"

Jonathan Kealing
(Former) Assistant Director, Media Strategy
The Lawrence Journal-World
Lawrence, Kan.

When I was covering the University of Kansas, I received a package in the mail. It had a bunch of stamps on it — was very strange-looking. I had a busy day. I set it aside until the end of the day.

Later, I picked it up, looked inside it and realized that in the mail I had received a great number of confidential student documents that were being thrown into recycling for anyone to recover, and they included Social Security numbers, student ID numbers — all sorts of information.

So I started making some calls — talked to the university. They were very upset, very defensive. They wanted the information back; said there wasn't a story; said we had no business having them, etcetera. The university tried to make the story about us — us refusing to give them the documents back. But we persevered, pressed through, published. It became a major story around the region and the university made changes — locked bins, instituted policies for handling confidential student information, offered credit checks to the people whose information had been made available.

Really seeing how the university changed because of that story, because of the work that we had done, it was really powerful because it's something that had a positive change for our community. We were able to see that positive change, very quickly, because of the story that we did and the reporting.

I would walk around offices up on campus for the next couple of weeks, and I would see new shredders coming out of boxes all the time.

Because everyone had gotten the memo that you're going to treat these documents properly, you're going to treat them with care, because people's lives and livelihoods could be damaged if you mishandle them. Watching them do that, watching the contracts that they signed to properly handle and dispose of these documents was really heartwarming because it did hold a large institution accountable. It made a positive change that really helped make our audience's life better.

HD video: http://www.whoneedsnewspapers.org/np_interviews.php?npld=epiphany &ivld=epiphany091

Jonathan Kealing is director, interactive properties at Public International in Minneapolis. Previously, he was The Lawrence Journal-World assistant director of media strategy. In this role, he helped launch and nurture some of the company's innovative sites such as WellCommons and Sunflower Horizons. He also helped ensure the continued growth, in traffic and interaction as well as revenue, for LJWorld.com, KUsports.com and lawrence.com. His primary focus was helping the staff engage the community via their websites and social media, and on creating interactive, multimedia journalism, which promoted website growth.

Section V

EMBRACING EMPATHY

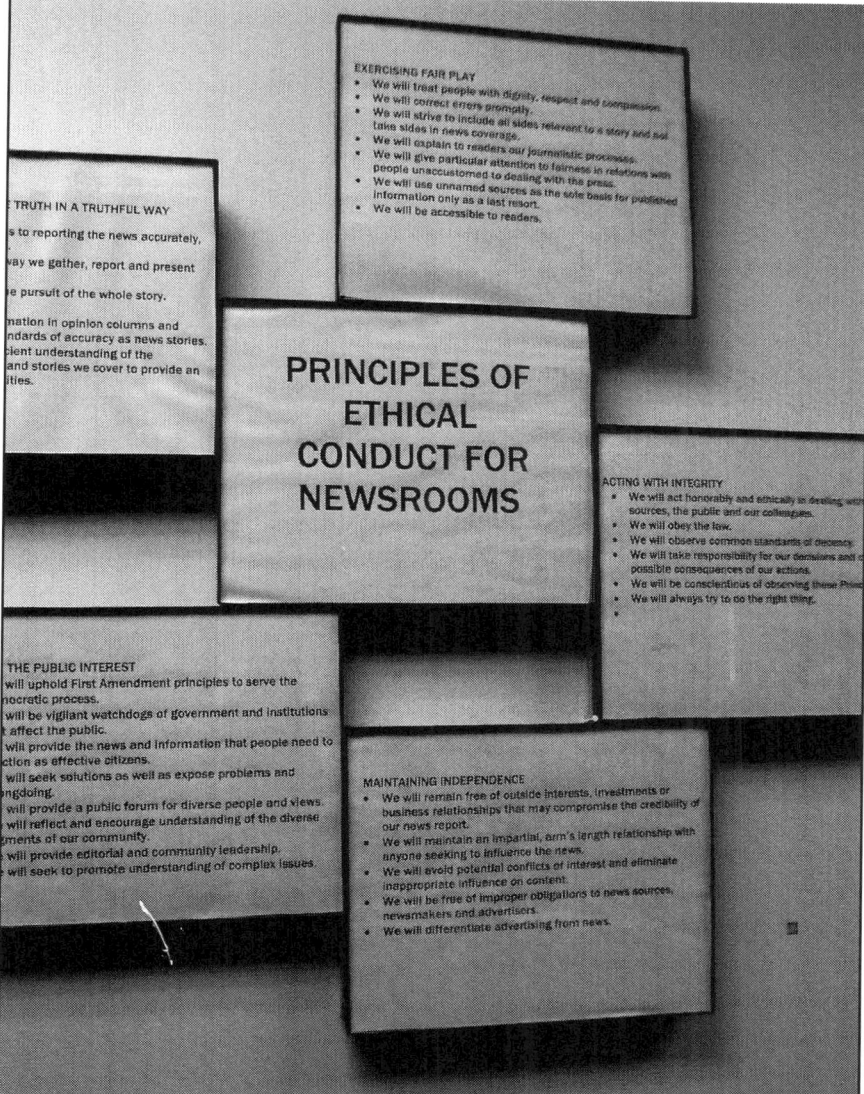

EXERCISING FAIR PLAY
- We will treat people with dignity, respect and compassion.
- We will correct errors promptly.
- We will strive to include all sides relevant to a story and not take sides in news coverage.
- We will explain to readers our journalistic processes.
- We will give particular attention to fairness in relations with people unaccustomed to dealing with the press.
- We will use unnamed sources as the sole basis for published information only as a last resort.
- We will be accessible to readers.

TRUTH IN A TRUTHFUL WAY

to reporting the news accurately,

way we gather, report and present

pursuit of the whole story.

nation in opinion columns and
ndards of accuracy as news stories.
cient understanding of the
and stories we cover to provide an
ities.

PRINCIPLES OF ETHICAL CONDUCT FOR NEWSROOMS

ACTING WITH INTEGRITY
- We will act honorably and ethically in dealing with sources, the public and our colleagues.
- We will obey the law.
- We will observe common standards of decency.
- We will take responsibility for our decisions and possible consequences of our actions.
- We will be conscientious of observing these Prin
- We will always try to do the right thing.

THE PUBLIC INTEREST
will uphold First Amendment principles to serve the
mocratic process.
will be vigilant watchdogs of government and institutions
affect the public.
will provide the news and information that people need to
ction as effective citizens.
will seek solutions as well as expose problems and
ngdoing.
will provide a public forum for diverse people and views.
will reflect and encourage understanding of the diverse
ments of our community.
will provide editorial and community leadership.
will seek to promote understanding of complex issues.

MAINTAINING INDEPENDENCE
- We will remain free of outside interests, investments or business relationships that may compromise the credibility of our news report.
- We will maintain an impartial, arm's length relationship with anyone seeking to influence the news.
- We will avoid potential conflicts of interest and eliminate inappropriate influence on content.
- We will be free of improper obligations to news sources, newsmakers and advertisers.
- We will differentiate advertising from news.

Embracing Empathy

A common code of neutrality and disengagement runs deep through journalism education and journalism practice. But sometimes humanity shatters the code.

Reporters are taught to avoid engagement with their subjects in order to avoid conflicts of interest and for their own sanity. But sometimes reporters who cover their communities realize that offering a helping hand is more compelling than maintaining professional distance. Serving the public remains the prime goal for these journalists, but acknowledging the circumstances they are encountering — by treating people with empathy, respect and, occasionally, a helping hand — does not impede them from keeping their communities well and fairly informed.

In this section, professional journalists reveal moments when they shelved the code of disengagement because of situations they faced, and they explain what they learned in the process.

"I Was the Conduit"

Dennis Anderson
(Former) Managing Editor
The Lawrence Journal-World
Lawrence, Kan.

There are probably several stories I could tell, but there's one that always hits home. It was early in my career. A boy had drowned in a pool, and it was my job to tell that story. So I called up their home, and I talked to the boy's mother.

I've called other people related to that. Sometimes people just hang up on you. In this case the mother talked, and talked and talked. I got a sense that she had a story to tell about her son — a young boy — about who that boy was, and I was the conduit. I was a person telling the community about this boy, and I was able to do that.

I knew, after I hung up the phone, that I helped her. I helped her through something that was very difficult for her and her family.

We can do a lot of things like that [to] help people. That's what I like about this job. Not every day is great. Not every day is it something you want to go home and tell your wife and family about. But there are days like that — when you can help people.

HD video: http://www.whoneedsnewspapers.org/np_interviews.php?npld=epiphany&ivld=epiphany090

Dennis Anderson joined The Lawrence Journal-World as managing editor in 2005. The Journal-World won three consecutive Associated Press Managing Editor Convergence Awards (2007–2009). In July 2012, Anderson was named executive editor at The Peoria Journal Star. Anderson is also a member of the Associated Press Managing Editors board of directors. Prior to joining The Journal-World, Anderson worked for Gannett Co., including serving as managing editor of The Norwich (Conn.) Bulletin from 1999–2005 and as metro editor of The Binghamton (N.Y.) Press & Sun-Bulletin from 1996–1999. He was recognized as one of Gannett's top 10 supervisors in 2000, and in 2006 won the Kansas Press Association's award for Best Column Writing.

"What Was Happening to Their Children"

Mike Arnholdt
(Former) Executive Editor
The Fayetteville Observer
Fayetteville, N.C.

Some of our coverage area is Fort Bragg — one of the biggest military bases in the world. There are about 50,000 soldiers at Fort Bragg. And, since 2001, the soldiers at Fort Bragg have been continually involved in the wars in Iraq and Afghanistan.

We have — at least a dozen times — sent a reporter and photographer team into these countries embedded with those soldiers to tell their stories and, of course, we run those stories in the paper. But we also post them on our website.

It has been touching to hear from the families of these soldiers — across the country — who will tell us that if it weren't for our paper, they wouldn't have any idea what was happening to their children.

HD video: http://www.whoneedsnewspapers.org/np_interviews.php?npld=epiphany&ivld=epiphany042

Mike Arnholdt was named executive editor at The Fayetteville Observer in 2009. He joined The Fayetteville Times in 1978, working as a copy editor, copy desk chief and features and was named managing editor when The Times and Observer were merged. Arnholt came to Fayetteville in 1974 as a soldier reassigned from South Korea to Fort Bragg, where he served with a public information detachment in the 1st Corps Support Command. Arnholdt retired from The Observer in 2012.

"Find Some Hope"

Charlotte Atkins
(Former) Editor-in-Chief
The Rome News-Tribune
Rome, Ga.

We had a week here in Rome, Ga., where it was just rife with tragedy. We had a seemingly random murder; we had a mother who killed herself and her two kids. There was a homeless gentleman found dead in the river, and there were other things along the periphery. Then on Thursday, two people were arrested — the man's wife and his best friend were implicated in his murder. Those families each had three kids, so we had four very high-profile deaths in our community that rocked schools and rocked churches.

You usually don't have just that back-to-back-to-back, big tragic breaking news here.

There was a point in my career here when I would've said, "Wow, what a front page — all this breaking front page news." The truth is, in that moment, I realized people were going to read every word of our front page, and they were going to feel awful. My mission to my staff that day was to find some hope. They looked at me a little bit crazy. I said, "All these stories involve children — children whose lives have been wrecked in one way or the other." I said, "Go find me some hope. Find something that says there are kids in Rome, Ga., who still live these happy, untainted lives."

Someone came back and said, "We've got a 5 year old, singing the national anthem at the Rome Braves game." I said, "Great. Go get a photo and interview her." And they're like: "Interview a 5 year old?" I said, "Yes, she got picked for that."

I remember that front page. Across the top we had that headline about the arrest; down the side was a story about the mother who was terminally ill with cancer, and that's why she killed herself and her kids. And in the middle of all this chaos in our community was a cute little blonde girl singing the national anthem at our local ballpark, and just a short story about how she auditioned, and she got it.

We didn't have to blow out the news to make people read those other stories. But I needed to show one child, who was going forth in life and happy. On this day I didn't go for a big blowout package on the arrest. I didn't go for a big blowout package on the mother who killed herself and her kids. Those stories didn't need any help being big stories. People were going to read them.

After people read our front page, they were going to be demoralized and heartbroken. I don't know how much impact having that little girl in the middle of all that mattered, but I like to think it mattered. I wouldn't say it was great journalism. It was just perspective.

HD video: http://www.whoneedsnewspapers.org/np_interviews.php?npld=epiphany&ivld=epiphany046

Charlotte Atkins became the editor of the Rome News-Tribune in 2004. She previously worked at The Columbus (Ga.) Ledger-Enquirer as metro editor; The Monterey (Calif.) County Herald as assistant metro editor, news editor, online editor and associate editor; a decade at The Vero Beach (Fla.) Press-Journal as a government and political reporter, photographer and lifestyle editor and a stint as director of a live daily television talk show in Florida. In 2011, Atkins became executive director of Cancer Navigators, a nonprofit organization in Rome, Ga. She won numerous awards for investigative journalism, news and feature writing, headline writing, photography and newspaper design. Atkins is an Auburn University graduate.

"That Emotionally Affected Me ... We Were All Just Very Innocent about These Things"

John Bodette, executive editor
The St. Cloud Times
St. Cloud, Minn.

A mom and dad in our community came in and said that their daughters were missing, and they were very concerned about it — it was Fred and Rita Reker. I remember talking to them and seeing the pain and anguish they had. Then, shortly after that, they found out that the two girls had been abducted and slain. They found them in a quarry, nearby, and I knew how difficult it was.

We did the story about the missing girls, and then we did the story about when authorities found them. It was just so emotional to hear the story of what Fred and Rita were going through. That remains an unsolved slaying.

Another example would be the Jacob Wetterling abduction in the late '80s. He was abducted while he was biking with his brother and another child coming back from a video store about 9 at night in St. Joseph (Minn.) — a small town. That remains unsolved. That emotionally affected me because it was at a time maybe when we were all just very innocent about these things.

What Patty Wetterling and her family — Jerry and Patty Wetterling went through — we covered that wall-to-wall and continue to. The world is out of sync until we find out what happened to Jacob.

HD video: http://www.whoneedsnewspapers.org/np_interviews.php?npId=epiphany &ivId=epiphany096

John Bodette started his journalism career in 1974 as wire editor at The St. Cloud Times. He also served as city editor and news editor. He was named managing editor at The Times in 1986 and executive editor Dec. 23, 2005. In 1981, he was one of the original journalists on the prototype project that helped create USA Today. Bodette is a past president of the Minnesota Associated Press Managing Editors Association. He was the winner of the 2008 Robert G. McGruder Award for Diversity Leadership. Bodette is a graduate of St. John's University, Collegeville, Minn. To relax, he runs triathlons, duathlons, half marathons and marathons — none of them very fast.

"When You Write ... People's Lives Change"

Rob Curley
(Former) Senior Editor, Digital
The Las Vegas Sun
Las Vegas, Nev.

When I was covering politics at The Topeka Cap-ital-Journal, I realized that when you write these stories, people's lives change. Somebody might get voted out of office because of something that you reported on. You realized that as you are writing there were real implications to this.

I remember when one of the first times this hit me — it was very pow-erful, and I was also very young, and it was very sad for me too because a person I had written about called me, crying, and I felt horrible. That wasn't what I was trying to accomplish at all, and I realized I just had to be very responsible about this power.

It sounds really stupid, but you know the *Spider-Man* movie: With awesome power comes awesome responsibility.

I felt at that moment that I had better be on my game.

I also remember the first time I realized a person's relationship with a newspaper was different from what I thought it was. It was the whole experience of the newspaper that was important. Not just my stories, but also the crossword puzzle — even how the newspaper was delivered.

I was at The Ottawa (Kan.) Herald; I loved it. I was at a grocery store, and a woman recognized me, and I thought, "Oh, my God, this is like the greatest thing ever." She says, "You work at The Ottawa Herald, don't you?" I said, "I do." And she says, "I been wanting to talk to you." And I said, "Let's talk." And she says, "You guys used to put the paper on the sidewalk, and now it's more in the driveway. How do I get it back more in the sidewalk where I liked it?"

That's when I realized this relationship is much more than my writing. I mean there's a whole other thing going on here that I don't get. It was very powerful for me that I had grown up loving journalism, loved writing, and she didn't want to talk about that — she wanted to know why the paper wasn't closer to her door.

HD video: http://www.whoneedsnewspapers.org/np_interviews.php?npId=epiphany&ivId=epiphany068

Rob Curley was senior editor of the new-media division of the Las Vegas Sun and Greenspun Media Group; subsequently he was hired by The Orange County Register in 2012. Curley had joined Greenspun in June 2008. Prior to heading to Las Vegas, Curley was vice president of product development at Washington Post. Newsweek Interactive for two years and director of new media and convergence for The Naples Daily News and its sister publications along Florida's Gulf Coast. From 2002 to 2004, Curley held management positions in the interactive operations and editorial departments for The Lawrence (Kan.) Journal-World. He gained national attention when he became one of the first online editors in the nation chosen to lead a news organization's entire print and broadcast news operations. From 2000 to 2002, Curley was new media director for The Topeka (Kan.) Capital-Journal. In 2001 the Newspaper Association of America named Curley the industry's New Media Pioneer of the Year, making him the youngest person to win the award. Curley's groundbreaking work has been documented in college journalism textbooks, industry and mainstream magazines and white papers and on NPR's "Morning Edition."

"You Have to Be a Human Being, Too"

Michael Days, editor
The Philadelphia Daily News
Philadelphia, Pa.

I was an intern at The Minneapolis Tribune, and as an intern you got sent out to do a cute little story sometimes. Well, this story turned out to be about a family of six who was living in a car in Minneapolis in the wintertime. I spent time with them — talked to all the kids, talked to the mom, talked to the father.

You talk about ethics — I probably broke some rule there, because I just wasn't comfortable taking their time, writing this story, without giving them something. I had a $20 bill in my pocket, and I gave it to them. You know at Missouri [School of Journalism] we were probably told not to do that, but sometimes you have to be a human being, too.

I wrote that story, and people just came out of the woodwork and helped them get housing and food and set them up. I guess, intellectually, I understood about the power of the pen before that point, but for me, personally, that was an important moment — that was a moving moment.

They tried to get help, they'd been to agencies and nobody could quite make it work for them. By putting that story in the paper, people came out — people helped them and got them settled in. So, for me, that was what was an important moment — and there have been many others over the years — but that was an important moment for me.

HD video: http://www.whoneedsnewspapers.org/np_interviews.php?npId=epiphany&ivId=epiphany005

Michael Days is an executive V.P. and editor of The Philadelphia Daily News. Since joining the paper 25 years ago he has served as managing editor, deputy managing editor and was named editor in 2005. Under his leadership the paper has won numerous awards, including the Pulitzer Prize for investigative reporting in 2010. Days earned a master's degree from the University of Missouri, School of Journalism. He is a McCormick Fellow and graduate of the Media Management Center's Advanced Executive Program at Northwestern University. He served on the APME national board and is editor of its quarterly magazine, *APME NEWS*.

"Everybody Is Treated as a 'Cover Person'"

Dennis Fujimoto
Chief Photographer and Columnist
The Garden Island
Lihue, Kauai, Hawaii

My first job was with The Garden Island. I was in the fifth grade. I didn't know really what I wanted to be. I learned photography when I was in high school through a home study course, and everybody was going to college, so I said: OK, I know how to do photography. Why don't I do journalism? That's how I started.

I was offered a job with *TV Guide* magazine. *TV Guide*, at that time, was owned by Walter Annenberg. He had this phenomenal staff. And this one guy — what really stuck in my mind is the fact that he told me, "It doesn't matter whether your subject has six million dollars in his pocket and you only have six cents. You're just as good as him." I never forgot that.

We used to go to lunch and these aspiring performers would come up to us and want to be on the cover of *TV Guide* [saying]: "Can you get me on the cover? Get me on the cover."

Last week I went to Little League baseball. You see all these little kids come up. It's not just: "I wanna be on the front page now." It's: "I wanna be on the front page. I wanna be in color."

There's a parallel there, you know. I'm working with these kids — but that's how the movie performers were when I worked for *TV Guide*. Everybody wanted a cover. So everybody is treated as [though he or she is] a "cover person." Like that guy said: "Whether you got six million dollars and the other guy has got six cents — everybody's equal."

HD video: http://www.whoneedsnewspapers.org/np_interviews.php?npId=epiphany &ivId=epiphany072

Dennis Fujimoto has been in the news gathering business from an early age. He started collecting informative tidbits in elementary school where English replaced pidgin. In the fifth grade, he covered Pop Warner games for the newspaper. In high school, he honed his photographic skills and selected journalism as a career because it complemented his interest in photography. His first job out of college was with the *TV Guide*, which allowed him to travel extensively. He's been the primary photographer at The Garden Island for over 20 years.

"Sometimes Being There for Somebody Is ... Important"

Tom Gorman
Senior Editor, Print
The Las Vegas Sun
Las Vegas, Nev.

When I was working at The Los Angeles Times, I got a call one morning that there had been a car accident in the mountains above Los Angeles involving six teenagers in a car that had gone over the side. All six were killed. They were leaving a rave — an overnight kind of concert. I don't know what caused the accident, but all six were killed, and it happened on my beat.

I had to go knock on the doors of five of the homes of the teenagers who died. I chose to be vulnerable, and [the parents] opened up their teenagers' scrapbooks and their yearbooks and shared them with me. They needed immediately to talk to somebody. Whether it was cathartic or just wanting to share these memories — I would spend an hour or more letting them talk to me about their children who had just died the night before.

I shared my concerns — as a father raising a teenage daughter who had been skydiving — [about] how quickly life can go.

I think that story showed me that journalism is a lot more than going to a city council meeting or interviewing Grace Slick or covering an election. You touched the lives of people, and there are times when you need to let down your mask as a reporter who is not interested. There are times when you don't need to be neutral. You can be sympathetic or you can be angry. The humanity of the reporter needs to come out.

I think that's when I realized that a big part of what a reporter brings to the profession is not just coolness — [situations] when you need to be cool and calculating in terms of what to write. You also need to bring compassion and empathy to be supportive. Sometimes being there for somebody is as important as getting the story and walking out with something in your notebook.

That day I went home exhausted — emotionally drained — and my wife hugged me. It was tough, but that's when I realized a journalist touches a lot of lives.

HD video: http://www.whoneedsnewspapers.org/np_interviews.php?npId=epiphany &ivId=epiphany067

Tom Gorman joined The Sun in 2005 from The Los Angeles Times, where his 32-year career spanned local, state and national reporting before moving to the metro editing desk. Gorman was hired at The Sun as a metro columnist. To qualify for a covered parking spot with precious shade, he became an editor, and in December 2009 was named senior editor, print. He has a degree from Cal State Fullerton.

"He Was as Important as the President of the United States"

Henry M. Lopez
(Former) Digital Development Manager and Project Manager
The Santa Fe New Mexican
Santa Fe, N.M.

A lot of folks in the newsrooms don't like writing obituaries, but I actually did. When those assignments would come up, I wanted them.

I had just come to Santa Fe from California and went to write about the death of a young man. I went to his family's home, and I sat in their kitchen, and it looked a whole lot like my own grandmother's kitchen. We talked for two-and-a-half hours about their son. At the end of it, the mother was in tears and thanking me for coming out because someone cared. And she handed me a big sack of frozen green chilies. If you're in New Mexico, you know that nothing says love like a bag of green chilies.

I just remember going home that night, and thinking how important it was to these folks that their son was being written about in the newspaper. For that day, when that story ran in the newspaper, he was as important as the president of the United States. I know they kept that newspaper.

People don't clip websites the way they do a newspaper. You knew that they had a real emotional connection with this newspaper and the newspaper in general.

That — and similar experiences writing obituaries — those were my aha moments — when it comes to family.

HD video: http://www.whoneedsnewspapers.org/np_interviews.php?npId=epiphany
&ivId=epiphany064

Henry M. Lopez was the manager of digital development for Santafenewmexican.
com. He focused on developing digital business opportunities for The New Mexican by reaching across traditional organizational lines. Lopez was a former web
editor and reporter for the newspaper, and he has taught multimedia journalism
online and at industry conferences and fellowships. He is now owner of Lopez
Webworks in Santa Fe.

"That Made Things in Perspective"

David Raese, co-owner and publisher
The Dominion Post
Morgantown, W.V.

I used to cover high school sports in this town, and we had a longtime football coach that even when I went to school he was the football coach — and then when I was covering sports, I covered his teams. We had a good relationship because he knew me and my brothers. Every once in a while I'd have to take him to task in my column for something, but we'd get to an understanding.

He died of a heart attack, which was a bit sudden — he was not that old and seemed to be in good shape. So I went to the funeral home, and the wife was there and their son was there, and he was probably maybe middle school age. I just expressed how sorry I was. They told me after he died they went home, and they went through a box of old clippings. They found a column that I had written when the boy was younger and I was doing an interview with the coach after they'd lost a football game. We were discussing the football game, and the boy came running up and grabbed his dad, and I put a note in the column about how that made things in perspective. They were reading that column to soothe themselves during that time.

Now that told me you can make a difference. It doesn't have to be a law changed or anything else. But in someone's life — you get it down to that level. I thought that made a difference, and I've always remembered that.

HD video: http://www.whoneedsnewspapers.org/np_interviews.php?npId=epiphany &ivId=epiphany003

David Raese has been publisher of The Dominion Post since 1987. He is a lifetime resident of Morgantown, W.V. Raese is part owner and president of the board of directors of the West Virginia Newspaper Publishing Co. and part owner of Greer Industries. He was the 2002 Campaign Chair of the United Way of Monongalia and Preston Counties and is an active member of the Rotary Club of Morgantown. Raese is married to Kathleen Raese and has four children: Rebecca, Ethan, Adam and Isabel.

Section VI

PRACTICING JOURNALISM

Practicing Journalism

Journalism's hurdles to entry are lower, but mastering the craft of journalism resembles mastering the *practice* of medicine and law. Just as lawyers and doctors perfect their skills through experience, journalism skills are fine-tuned in the field. Professional journalists hone their skills: They observe events, collect facts, interview people and decide what needs to be communicated. And, as the digital technology of journalism evolves, they integrate new media techniques into their arsenal of reporting tools.

In classrooms or as apprentices, professional journalists learn pragmatic and ethical guidelines for these tasks. Journalists use this knowledge, and temper it with their experience and critical-thinking skills, to produce each day's diet of news. Subsequently, they absorb feedback, evaluate the results and repeat these procedures — tempered by the effects of their previous work.

In this section, professional journalists share personal epiphanies that profoundly altered their practice of the craft of journalism.

"You Can Tell Good Stories in Any Medium"

Jim Alred, new media director
The Rome News-Tribune
Rome, Ga.

In 2004–2005, at The Naples (Fla.) Daily News, I had been doing multimedia journalism for about six months. Vonzell Solomon, a woman from Fort Myers, Fla., made the final three of the "American Idol" contest. When you make the final three of the "American Idol" you go home, and you get to perform in front of a hometown crowd. At that time, the editor of The Daily News and the publisher weren't real sure that video meant anything. And Solomon was actually a story they had completely ignored. They basically said The Fort Myers News-Press had sent someone out to Hollywood to cover her. We didn't get to interview her, but I got her performing at Fort Myers. Came back to the newspaper and posted it.

The servers for Scripps Howard — Naples was a Scripps Howard newspaper — were based in Knoxville, Tenn. I got a call from Knoxville, and it was like: "What did you do?" I said, "What are you talking about?" "Our servers are about to go down. We're going to have to put you on a separate server just for traffic."

Turns out The [Fort Myers] News-Press didn't have video of Vonzell Solomon. We had almost 55,000 views and plays of the video in less than a day and a half. I got called into the editor's office the next day, and he was like: "What happened?" I said, "I told you this was big."

"But more people saw that video than read our newspaper." I said,

"Yes, you're right. We're not always going to get that with every video, but if you ignore this storytelling medium, you're going to start ignoring a whole lot of people's interests."

If you can tell good stories in any medium you're going to be doing well, and I thought that was a moment when I convinced a lot of people that was the case.

HD video: http://www.whoneedsnewspapers.org/np_interviews.php?npld=epiphany &ivld=epiphany047

Jim Alred is the new media director for the News Publishing Company in Rome, Ga. He oversees Internet operations for the company's websites and directs the multimedia department. Before returning to his hometown of Rome, he was an on-line editor and online videographer at The Naples (Fla.) Daily News. At The News-Tribune, Alred and his crew have won awards from the Inland Press Association, Southern Newspaper Publisher Association and the Georgia Press Association for website and multimedia excellence. They produced the first newspaper produc-tions to receive Southeast Regional Emmy nominations. Alred began his career as sports editor for The Selma (Ala.) Times Journal after graduating from Auburn University.

"Something Citizen Journalism Just Couldn't Emulate"

Michael Becker, city/web editor
The Bozeman Daily Chronicle
Bozeman, Mont.

I wasn't working here at the paper at the time; this was during the period when I was away. But we had, in 2009, early March, a gas explosion downtown. Several buildings — part of a block downtown — exploded; one woman was killed. This happened shortly after 8 in the morning. Thankfully, downtown wasn't very busy yet.

From my office, where I was monitoring Twitter that day, I started to see reports from local people that I was following about what happened downtown.

There was a loud explosion. Then the reports started becoming clearer, clearer and clearer as to what happened. Throughout the day people volunteered their time to be on their computers and relay valuable information.

At the same time my wife, who was working for the paper, had of her own volition started The Bozeman Daily Chronicle's Twitter account. And on that day it went from having a very small modest number of followers to having a lot of followers as she began to become the conduit for information.

We all wrote blog posts about it. We were very ideological about what happened that day because we were fresh in the afterglow of what we thought was this big revolution in journalism. That this was citizen journalism at its best, right?

I saw that day that despite what all the citizens were saying — and it was valuable, they were putting out good information — it wasn't until the next day's paper that I really understood that it took a newspaper to bring it all together into a place where people would consume it, consider it and learn from it.

People watching Twitter that day and in the couple of days afterward, as the pieces started to get picked up downtown, they would've gotten snatches of the story. They would've gotten lots of links. And, for some people, that's enough.

But when the paper ran a huge front-page photo, that was so big it went below the fold (of an aerial shot of this devastation) and then packaged five or seven stories written by reporters who were scrambling around like mad that day, and covered the Twitter side of it, that packaging really made me understand that this hectic conglomeration of how a newspaper comes together every day — online and in print — was something that citizen journalism, at the time, just couldn't emulate.

That guided me. It set me off on a steep and thorny learning curve reading about this stuff, so that my passion and ideas about citizen journalism have been tempered a little bit. I still think it's very valuable. But I also think that it takes a newspaper — or at least paid journalists — to do the best job.

HD video: http://www.whoneedsnewspapers.org/np_interviews.php?npId=epiphany&ivId=epiphany082

Michael Becker joined The Chronicle in 2005 and became web editor in 2009. In addition to his work for the paper, he has taught writing to college freshman, edited doctoral dissertations, written for magazines and worked as a science reporter. His interest in online journalism grew out of a fascination with blogs and hypertext in the early 2000s and out of the certainty that web technology could be used to tell important stories in interesting ways. Becker is a graduate of Montana State University with a master's degree in English. He lives in Bozeman with his partner, Susan, taking care of his two sons and a few dozen blogs and websites.

"It Was Just a Very Grim Scene"

Felice Belman, editor
The Concord Monitor
Concord, N.H.

When I started at The Monitor, I was a news reporter. I didn't have any particular beat when I first got here, and one day I came to work and a young boy had disappeared. He had been swimming with some friends and presumably had drowned, but they couldn't find him. So I was sent out to cover this thing.

It was awful. They had the Fish and Game Department divers looking for him, and his family was on one bank and the friends — 11- and 12-year-old boys — they were waiting on the bank of the river.

The day went on and on and on. It was just a very grim scene. I had never covered anything tragic like that, and I was sort of paralyzed by it. I had in my head that a decent person would not disturb these mourning families, so I didn't approach the family of the missing boy — who did turn up dead — or his friends or the parents of the friends. I wrote a very wooden account from officialdom, and I thought I had done the right thing.

I came in the next morning and got screamed at by the parents of the dead boy who said, "We saw you there. You saw us. You never approached us. How dare you presume to write about our son without even talking to us? We wanted to tell you about him and you blew us off essentially." I was stunned by that. I sat down with them and a whole roomful of this kid's friends and ended up writing what I should've done in the first place, which was a story about this kid — not just about the Fish and Game divers.

That's not the reaction you would get from everybody, but to me it was a powerful lesson. You always try. You always do the hard thing. Maybe it'll work; maybe it won't. But you avoid that at your peril because there was such a human story there, and it took me two tries to get it right.

These were people who appreciated what The Monitor could do for them, which was allow them to talk about their son. Not everybody will do that, but they wanted to and I was to be their conduit, and I had blown it. So that's going to stay with me forever.

I've gotten tougher about those kind of stories. It's not so hard now to make that awful phone call. And it's easy for me to encourage young reporters to do those hard things because I've gone through it.

HD video: http://www.whoneedsnewspapers.org/np_interviews.php?npld=epiphany &ivld=epiphany012

Felice Belman is editor of The Concord Monitor, where she has worked, off and on, for more than 20 years as an editor and, before that, a state politics reporter. Among her brief forays elsewhere, she also spent two years as Maryland politics editor at The Washington Post. Belman is the coeditor, with Mike Pride, of "The New Hampshire Century," a collection of profiles of 100 notable state figures from the 20th century. She twice served as a juror for the Pulitzer Prizes. Belman graduated from Oberlin College in 1988.

"What You Do Has Broad Effects on People's Lives"

Thomas Dewell, coeditor
The Jackson Hole News & Guide
Jackson, Wyo.

I was a court reporter — you've got to decide if you're going to use this or not — and this really opened my mind to the power of journalism.

I was a court reporter, sitting in the justice of the peace court, and a woman I knew had come in for her second DUI, and I was talking to her. She was very nervous. She offered a sex act to me if I would not put it in the newspaper — [put] her DUI in the newspaper — because she didn't want her family to know about it. I told her, I couldn't do that, and that maybe her family should know about it if it had gotten that bad. That's when I realized: Wow — what you do has broad effects on people's lives! And what people will do — or won't do — to change the course of that.

HD video: http://www.whoneedsnewspapers.org/np_interviews.php?npld=epiphany&ivld=epiphany084

Thomas Dewell serves as coeditor for the News & Guide and managing editor for The Daily. He also contributes stories and photos, designs and copy edits pages and posts stories to the web. He serves on the business' marketing council and website design and implementation team. He is a past president of the Wyoming Press Association and current member of the Wyoming Press Association Foundation board. A graduate of University of California, Santa Barbara, Dewell started in newspapers as an intern at The Santa Barbara Independent. At The Jackson Hole Guide, he climbed from reporter to editor. He became a partner and coeditor when The News & Guide merged in 2002. His volunteer work includes helping Spanish-speaking middle school students with their studies. He lives in Wilson, Wyo., with his family, and (in 2011) two horses, two cats, a dog and 12 chickens.

"Yes, I Know How to Do This Now"

Bennie DiNardo
Deputy Managing Editor, Multimedia
The Boston Globe
Boston, Mass.

When I took my first full-time job, I was still surrounded by doubts like: Who am I to say that I am a journalist?

I wrote a story about a man who was an insurance agent who had swindled people. It was one of those where he did not want to cooperate, and we had to go knock on his door and the photographer was behind me and got a picture of him as he was opening the door and was closing it again.

It wasn't so much the impact of that story, but that all the pieces came together — that I was able to tell it. I could describe the person in a way that people could understand with the right detail and the right anecdotes to bring that home to the audience. And I said, "Oh, so this is how it works." Before that, I was struggling to write, and I can remember, that morning, feeling: Yes, I know how to do this now.

There were some other stories following that about an investigation in the town of Auburn — into the police department where there was a lot of pent-up worry and anger and frustration and the folks who were concerned weren't able to get their story out, and I had tapped into a vein and all these people started talking to me. I realized the benefit that you can have when a third party comes in to tell a story who is not emotionally involved in either one of the sides or the parts of an issue.

So those kinds of experiences really brought home to me the sort of special role that journalism can play in a community.

HD video: http://www.whoneedsnewspapers.org/np_interviews.php?npId=epiphany&ivId=epiphany018

Bennie DiNardo became The Globe's deputy managing editor for multimedia in June 2008. In that position, he oversees the editorial operations of the Boston.com website and helps shape the newsroom's digital strategy, including the introduction of the paid bostonglobe.com website, introduced in 2011, and The Globe's video content. A Leominster, Mass., native, DiNardo has worked at The Globe since 1994. From 1999 to 2008 he served as The Globe's deputy business editor, responsible for day-to-day management of the business section. Previously, he was an assistant editor at the Globe Magazine and a copy editor. Before The Globe, DiNardo had been editor of The Boston Business Journal. A 1979 graduate of Cornell University, DiNardo received a master's degree from Yale Law School in 1986.

"It's Just a Wonderful Feeling"

David Farré, digital developer
The Burlington Free Press
Burlington, Vt.

I think a lot about my days at The Daily Targum (at Rutgers University), when I was just discovering the power of storytelling via daily newspapers. It just keeps coming back to mind.

One of my early assignments was working with a friend and reporter on a story about this black church in the very center of downtown New Brunswick [N.J.]. So we showed up on Sunday morning, [and] I took all these pictures. Having a camera [on assignment] for a newspaper — it just lets you walk into the middle of a scene in a way you would never do on your own. I just saw something I never would have seen otherwise.

Then back at the paper, when my friend was working on her story, she could see, over my shoulder, the pictures that were coming up on my screen. And she looked at one and said, "I wish I could write like that." That was sort of when it clicked for me — like wow. It's just a wonderful feeling to just make something like that — that speaks to someone so well.

HD video: http://www.whoneedsnewspapers.org/np_interviews.php?npId=epiphany&ivId=epiphany010

David Farré is the digital developer of The Burlington Free Press. He arrived in Vermont in July 2009 by way of Puerto Rico, his home; New Jersey, where he went to college; and Missouri, where he was the web editor of The Columbia Daily Tribune for eight years. You can follow him on Twitter @davidfarre.

"The Importance of Having an Authoritative, Responsible Source of Information"

Meg Heckman, (former) web editor
The Concord Monitor
Concord, N.H.

I'll go all the way back to the beginning. I was a senior at U.N.H. (University of New Hampshire), and I had ended up covering the police beat for the student paper. This was my first experience with hard news.

A couple of weeks into the first semester, a young woman on campus killed herself by jumping off the sixth or seventh floor of one of the high-rise dorms right in the middle of campus. Some boys on their way back from a party found her body. It was really terrible. The University barred most outside media after the first day, and rumors were flying, like crazy, all over the campus, and I was terrified to touch the story. The police agreed to talk to me and sat down — and the cop cried, and it was terrible, and I felt awful — and I wrote this story and talked to her friends.

A couple days after the story ran, we realized that the rumors had stopped. There was accurate information on campus. It didn't stop the tragedy, it didn't make it any easier, but it at least made everybody's grief process cleaner or at least allowed them to mourn accurate facts. That was when I realized the importance of having an authoritative, responsible source of information in a community. I've seen that type of thing time and time again. So when I read about staff cuts and pay cuts and reporters getting fired, it scares me. Because who is going to be that source of information?

HD video: http://www.whoneedsnewspapers.org/np_interviews.php?npld=epiphany &ivld=epiphany013

Meg Heckman is a former reporter who focuses heavily on digital and hyper-local coverage. She joined The Monitor newsroom in 2002 and covered city hall, the New Hampshire State House and two presidential primaries. Heckman attended the University of New Hampshire and has completed fellowships with the Poynter Institute for Media Studies and the New York Times Foundation. She is the co-author of "We Went to War: New Hampshire Remembers WWII" and has been honored by state and regional press associations. Heckman is currently a graduate assistant at Northeastern University. Her research interests include the role of women in emerging news organizations.

"For Reporters Who Were Too Big for an Assignment"

Tom Heslin
(Former) Senior V.P. and Editor
The Providence Journal
Providence, R.I.

I was a reporter at a great weekly newspaper in Kennebunk, Maine. I thrived there, and I had some success and I really became a little bit full of myself.

So one day the managing editor — who really had my number — said, "Tom, come here. We just got a call from a farmer out in West Kennebunk. He said his hen has laid the biggest egg that he has ever seen. Go out there and talk to this guy." My blood was boiling — but I said OK.

I came to this little glen with this little small farmhouse, and I knocked on the door, and this fellow invited me into the kitchen. It was dark and kind of damp, and he reached under the table where there was a big Kentucky Fried Chicken bucket. It was too dark, and I said, "Let's go outside." So I asked, "Do you know which hen laid the egg?" He said, "No, I got a lot of hens, I don't know." It wasn't really kind of going anywhere. He was: "Yeah ... No ... I don't know."

We put the bucket on the picnic table outside, and he was moving this tissue paper — gift-wrapping — and he reaches in and pulls out the egg. I take a picture of the egg, and as I click the shutter, I say, "OK, I quit." It was a good-size egg, but I went back to the office and met with the managing editor and said, "I quit — I'm not in a huff — I really can't do this anymore." I was kind of full of myself. I don't even know whether I ever did anything with the story.

Eventually we had a farewell celebration, and people gave me a copy of the egg picture, and we created The Royal Order of the Egg for reporters who were too big for an assignment, and it was a fun thing.

So, many years later, I was moving stuff around in my basement one day, and I opened up a box, and I got teary-eyed. The picture that I had taken of that egg — that framed picture of that egg — was there. What I saw — later on in my career at this point — was not the egg but the hand that was holding the egg. That hand was a workingman's hand. What I realized was what I hadn't thought to ask about him: What was his story? Where was his family? Did he ever have a day off? There were so many things I could've explored and probably found a wonderful career-defining story. I've told this many times.

When we go out and whether we're going to the simple assignments or going to see the big egg — let's remember: It's not about the egg — it's about the hand. That's my aha moment.

HD video: http://www.whoneedsnewspapers.org/np_interviews.php?npId=epiphany&ivId=epiphany022

Thomas E. Heslin became executive editor of The Providence Journal in November 2008. Prior to that, he was the managing editor for new media with responsibility for projo.com's online news initiatives. During that period, The Journal's website, projo.com, was acknowledged for excellence and innovation by the Associated Press Managing Editors, the Newspaper Association of America, the New England Associated Press News Executives, and *Editor & Publisher* magazine. Heslin helped found the New England First Amendment Coalition and ACCESS/RI, regional and state non-profit organizations dedicated to improving public awareness and access to the records and processes of government. He has served on the board of the national Freedom of Information Coalition, the Freedom of Information Committee of the American Society of News Editors (ASNE), and as a New England coordinator for the ASNE's Sunshine Week project on open government and freedom of information issues. Heslin retired from The Journal in April 2013 after 32 years of service.

"Something I Could Contribute to Directly"

**Christopher Mayer, (former) publisher
The Boston Globe
Boston, Mass.**

I started here in 1984, and I worked in the technology department back when it was called data processing. I had been tapped to accompany a reporter to Washington. There was an opportunity to get access to summary information from the government that would allow the newspaper and the Spotlight Team to do a story on money laundering.

Spending three weeks there, in DC, living out of a hotel room contributing to that made me realize that what we have for information and what we can do to keep people informed about what's going on [was] something I could contribute to directly. It didn't really occur to me exactly how coming to this institution with a degree in computer science was going to allow me to help do that, but at the end of the day it was meaningful.

Since then I have felt very strongly about the role that The Boston Globe plays and what every one of us as individuals can do to contribute.

HD video: http://www.whoneedsnewspapers.org/np_interviews.php?npId=epiphany &ivId=epiphany016

Christopher M. Mayer was publisher of The Boston Globe and the head of the New England Media Group at the time of this interview, both were subsidiaries of The New York Times Company. He is responsible for The Boston Globe and Boston.com; The Worcester Telegram & Gazette and GlobeDirect, the Globe's direct-mail subsidiary. Mayer also oversees the Company's investment in Metro Boston, a free daily newspaper. Mayer joined The Boston Globe in 1984 in the information services department. He was named senior vice president, circulation and operations in 2008, overseeing production, advertising operations, circulation marketing and distribution. Previously Mayer served as chief information officer and senior vice president, circulation, among other positions. Mayer received a B.S. in computer science from Yale University. He lives in South Boston with his wife and four children.

"I Could Have Done This Better"

Tim McDougall, V.P. and publisher
The Gazette Cedar
Rapids, Iowa

I've always believed in the power and purpose of journalism. That's one of the reasons I came here.

In our local option sales tax vote, which was about flood recovery, we covered that story and our lead city reporter expected the tax to pass pretty easily, as did most of the city leaders. But we were seeing a very heavy thread of comments in our articles that were highly, highly negative, and we were getting more and more of this negative thread. Mainly in the comments they were saying: You guys are not getting this point; you're missing this part of it. That was getting more and more vocal.

Now online commenters may be negative, so we don't want to treat their comments as scientific, but there was a much bigger groundswell of "anti" on this than we were giving it credit for. It was a very narrow vote. The tax lost by a couple hundred votes, so it was basically 50-50, but it lost.

Our writer Rick Smith — who's an excellent, veteran reporter — said he missed part of the story in the way he covered it. In hindsight, he said: I really didn't see this whole groundswell happening ... because there wasn't any leader or focus behind it, and it just started happening, and in the future I've got to find a different way to cover these things. We talked about how you embed yourself more in the community for that — because if you're more embedded, those things are more visible.

There may not have been tools 10 years ago for him to really be able to do that, as effectively, but there are much better tools now because of the way you can interact digitally and the speed you can interact with a large number of people. To hear Rick — who will self-admit he's one of the traditional guys around here — to hear Rick say: Boy, there's a different way I could have done this better. That was a big aha.

HD video: http://www.whoneedsnewspapers.org/np_interviews.php?npld=epiphany &ivld=epiphany094

Tim McDougall is V.P. of products for SourceMedia Group and publisher of The Gazette. Tim has spent over 20 years in multiple marketing disciplines, including packaged goods, sports marketing, agency management, new product development, retail marketing and media. McDougall's work with other companies includes Miller Brewing Company, the Houston Rockets, the New Orleans Hornets, GSD&M Advertising and the P. F. Chang's China Bistro Inc. restaurant group.

"You Can't Take Anything for Granted"

Mike Patrick, managing editor
The Coeur d'Alene Press
Coeur d'Alene, Idaho

I had just become the editor of a small daily in Southern Illinois — in fact, it was my hometown that I went back to. I knew everybody in town. My grandfather had been the judge, my mom had grown up there, and this was a town of about 6,000 people. I knew all the school board members, the superintendent of schools. I thought we had a great level of trust.

At a school board meeting that I didn't bother to advance, didn't ask tough questions, and there was virtually nobody from the community at this school board meeting, they had an executive session. They consolidated another school in the district, which just happened to have some of the best boys basketball players in the state of Illinois.

That was an aha moment for me. I work very hard to build respectful, trusting relationships with everybody I deal with, but that was a reminder that no matter how close you think you are with sources on a level of respect and honesty, you can't take anything for granted. It was a lesson that I've never forgotten.

HD video: http://www.whoneedsnewspapers.org/np_interviews.php?npld=epiphany &ivld=epiphany080

Mike Patrick, a native of St. Louis, is a University of Arizona journalism graduate who has worked at five daily newspapers: The Tucson Citizen (1980–81); The Arizona Daily Sun in Flagstaff (1981–82, 1984–1995); The Lawrenceville (Ill.) Daily Record (1982–84); The Provo (Utah) Daily Herald (1995–2001) and The Coeur d'Alene

Press (2001–present). At all those newspapers, except Tucson, he was managing editor or executive editor. In Provo, Patrick also served as general manager of the newspaper's website, harktheherald.com, and later as general manager of a newly acquired group of weeklies.

"A 'Defining Moment'"

Laurie Pfeifer
(Former) Managing Editor
The Aurora News-Register
Aurora, Neb.

One of the things that impacted me and made me realize the role that I could play, and particularly in balanced coverage, happened clear back when I was in college. It was when Robert Kennedy and Richard Nixon were running for president, and both of them made either whistle-stops or short visits to the community, and I was a dyed-in-the-wool Democrat. I was a Bobby Kennedy supporter all the way.

My professor gave me the assignment of covering Bobby Kennedy's whistle-stop at the train station, and I was ecstatic. But he said, by the way, you're also going to cover Richard Nixon, and your grade depends on your balanced coverage. It was probably the defining moment in my career. It made me realize it's not just a grade, you know, it's the information that you present to give a clear and balanced way of reporting.

So that was one of the defining moments in my development. It carried me through. I think about it a lot. Even if I fall on one side of an issue, I realize my personal feelings shouldn't come through. It's the accurate information that comes through.

HD video: http://www.whoneedsnewspapers.org/np_interviews.php?npId=epiphany &ivId=epiphany093

During her 38 years at The Aurora News-Register, **Laurie Pfeifer** served as feature editor, photographer, news editor and managing editor. Before joining The News-Register staff, she was a feature writer at The Fremont Tribune in Fremont, Neb. Pfeifer graduated from the University of Nebraska at Kearney in 1993 with a bachelor of science degree in journalism — comprehensive news/editorial. Pfeifer retired from The News Register in October 2013.

"Ask a Real Question"

Peter Phipps
Managing Editor for New Media
The Providence Journal
Providence, R.I.

There was a harness racetrack, and it was sort of a major taxpayer in this Ohio town. It had fallen on hard times. And one of the claims made was: People aren't going because they don't think they get a fair shake — that it's not quite on the up and up. So, I went and did a story.

There was this tipster who told us there was this guy who bets after the bell, and I went up and I caught him doing it. We had a photographer on the roof, and I had a phone, and I gave a little message, and I showed when the race started, and I showed when he bet — because I was watching him bet. He would line up, and then he would watch the TV, and he would know how these horses broke. So, I had it — it was wonderful — everything about it was wonderful.

But I didn't execute the final part of it. That was to go up to the guy and sit down with him and say, "Look, this is what I've got." — I was a kid — "This is what I've got. What am I to make of this?" Ask a real question, and then be quiet. The story suffered because of that. It would've been hard to do that.

As a kid, I would've had to be told to do that — I was maybe 30, something like that. An editor had to say, "No, no, no! This was all great, but now sit down and ask him a question: 'What's this all about?'" It would've been uncomfortable for me, but then it would've been so much better — to hear what he had to say about it. That would've been a higher level. It's a story I'm telling on myself, but I learned a lot from that.

HD video: http://www.whoneedsnewspapers.org/np_interviews.php?npld=epiphany &ivld=epiphany023

Peter Phipps has been with The Providence Journal since 1985, serving in a variety of writing and editing roles. The New England Associated Press named him best local columnist in 2001. From 2001–06, he served as Sunday editor, and since 2006, he has held key leadership roles in new media. He has been leader of a newsroom effort to create a paid-content model for projo.com. Phipps is a long distance runner, with 11 marathons and hundreds of other road races to his credit.

"It's Someone's Daughter, Someone's Mom"

Kevin G. Riley, (former) editor
The Dayton Daily News
Dayton, Ohio

My career was a little bit unusual because I didn't spend a lot of time as a reporter. I started as a copy editor and did a lot of things on the editing side. I kept wanting to be a reporter, and I kept getting told I was more valuable doing something else.

For a brief period I got to be a police reporter, which [was] really always my dream. My father was a police officer, and that's really what I always wanted to do. And just a couple weeks into it, I covered my first homicide. It was a great experience for me because I went and talked to the police lieutenant who gave the details. I was very comfortable in that situation. I'd been around cops my whole life, and what the guy had to say — how he described this victim, how she got herself in this spot — all made sense in the stereotypes I was used to.

I came back to the office, and I wrote up my story. And my editor said, "Well, you need to go talk to the victim's family." And I'm like: "Why? I mean this is like your standard homicide. I mean, cops said this. Why?" He said, "You need to go out there and talk to them."

So I drove out there — it was in kind of a rough neighborhood. I was a little bit lost. I was very intimidated, and I kept circling the block. I had made a decision to go back and tell my boss no one was home. At that moment, a woman came walking out of the house and waved me down. It turned out to be the victim's mom. She thought that I must be a cop or a building supervisor. I told her no — I was from the paper. And she talked to me for a few minutes.

What it taught me was: You read a lot of stories or you may write a lot of stories or you may hear a lot of stories about people being killed. But you should never forget — it's someone's daughter, someone's mom.

It's always stayed with me.

HD video: http://www.whoneedsnewspapers.org/np_interviews.php?npld=epiphany &ivld=epiphany001

Kevin G. Riley is the former editor of The Dayton Daily News and editor-in-chief for Cox Ohio Publishing's 12 newspapers and associated web sites. Riley was named editor in Dayton in January 2007. He had been deputy editor of The Dayton Daily News since September 2006, and served in many capacities for the newspaper since 1983, when he started his career while he was a student at the University of Dayton. After more than 27 years experience with Cox's Ohio properties, Riley was appointed editor of The Atlanta Journal-Constitution in January 2011. Riley has been named one of the industry's "20 Under 40" by the Newspaper Association of America. He was also a member of the association's Online Audience Development Committee and a mentor in its New Media Fellowship program. He has been a fellow at the University of Southern California's "Transforming News Organizations for the Digital Now," and he has attended Northwestern University's "Digital Strategies for Media Executives" conference.

"You Do It Because You Love It"

Pedro Rojas
(Former) Executive Editor
La Opinión
Los Angeles, Calif.

It was May 2006 [the March for Immigration Rights, downtown Los Angeles, May 1]. We assigned two reporters and one photographer because of so many marches that we have. I decided to go to the march just as a citizen, just to see what was going on. And it was enormous.

I called the publisher. Usually we have four pages of the editorial section that we pre-print. I called her and told her that this is huge. We need to do something extra. I said, "We should throw away that preprinted section and use those four pages, plus Section A, to make a huge statement with this."

On paper, we had three journalists. The next day, Sunday, we had six bylines: four were photographers because each one of them knew about the event and each one of them is a journalist. They came to cover the event without being assigned.

For me, this is what it is about. You do it because you love it. We didn't pay them extra because they came. Later, we had parties and things like that, but it was a testimony about what we do.

HD video: http://www.whoneedsnewspapers.org/np_interviews.php?npld=epiphany&ivld=epiphany068

Pedro Rojas was executive editor of La Opinión and a member of the company's executive committee. Rojas also supervised the daily's web page, which is one of the main content generators for the holding company ImpreMedia's portal site. Rojas is a seasoned journalist with more than 30 years experience in the newspaper business, the last 12 in upper management. From 2004 to 2005, Rojas served as executive editor at El Diario/La Prensa. In the recent years, La Opinión's journalists have received numerous awards from NAHP, NAHJ, NAM and others, including the @ Award for the best Spanish web page in 2007. Before joining La Opinión in 2003, Rojas worked at El Nuevo Dia for 27 years, in San Juan, Puerto Rico, the last six as managing editor. Rojas retired from La Opinión in July 2011.

"You're Only as Good as Your Sources"

Frank Scandale, (former) editor
The Record
Woodland Park, N.J.

Early on at The Daily Journal in Elizabeth (N.J.), I was covering a little town. I had a source on the town management team. He took a liking to me, and he was a good source of mine. He would give me the wink when he would come out for his bathroom break, and I'd have to go in the bathroom, and he would be in one stall, and he would feed me what's going on. So, I'm seeing how journalism works — sources and all that.

One day he calls me up, and he says, "Hey, I have a client that I want you to meet — I think it's a good story. You might want to meet him." So I say, "Well, OK. What's so special about him?" And he says, "He's running this restaurant now in this town, and he was a German immigrant — he came over and had nothing. He's got a good story." I said, "All right." He says, "Meet me down at his restaurant." So I go down there and I meet the guy, and he's nothing special. I can tell the story of just about anybody, but I couldn't figure out what was interesting about him — why he's unique — why I'd write about him.

So he left and my guy was fighting about the bill. And I said, "No, you can't pay." And he says, "No, no — don't worry about it." And I'm 22 or 23.

So I go back, and I got this great dilemma, and I said, "Well, what do I do with this?' I said, "I got this guy feeding me all these stories who's now put me in position to write about his client. So, he's kind of set me up on this, and if I don't write about his client — he's going to cut me off. And you're only as good as your sources."

People forget that in the '70s and '80s in New Jersey there were a lot of deals being made between the press and politicians. There was liquor coming in at Christmas time. There were rate cards for political columnists: $5 to write a good thing in a mention — $10 to write a bad thing about your opponent. This was going on. So I was really fretting. At the end of the day one of my editors said, "Well, it won't hurt anybody if you write it, right? Just do a soft puff piece." "Yeah," I said, "I know. But I don't feel right about it." So I didn't do it. I said, "No, I can't do it — I'm sorry — this just doesn't seem interesting." And he said, "OK." And that was it, and he still was my source. And I'm like: Oh — it's not a black-and-white thing — it's a negotiation along the way.

What it taught me was these are the rules of the road, so that I'm not compromised and I'm not making deals with people, and I don't owe anybody anything. I was happy it happened because — if I still tell that story 30 years later — it sounds like a great lesson that anybody can use.

HD video: http://www.whoneedsnewspapers.org/np_interviews.php?npld=epiphany &ivld=epiphany025

Frank Scandale was the editor of The Record from 2001–2011. Under his guidance, the paper earned The New Jersey Press Association's General Excellence Award for best newspaper in the state, seven of nine consecutive years. He led The Record's award-winning coverage of the September 11 attacks, which included the photo by Thomas Franklin of firemen raising the flag in front of the World Trade Center rubble. Scandale came to The Record from The Denver Post, where he served as assistant managing editor for news. He was previously the city editor for The Daily Journal in Elizabeth, N.J., and also held editorial positions at Reuters News. He is a 1979 graduate of Glassboro State College. In 2011, Scandale became V.P. of print production at Digital First Media, according to his Facebook log.

"There's Something Happening That We May Never See Again"

Richard Stein
Graphics/IT/Web Supervisor
The Garden Island
Lihue, Kauai, Hawaii

When I was in Pendleton, Ore., and I was working with The East Oregonian, I was their website producer, and the Pendleton Roundup was coming. We had lived there six, seven years before that, and I often went to the rodeo. So we had this opportunity to feed that rodeo into our website.

We said, "Let's get a video camera out there. Let's take some videos of this amazingly dramatic and exciting rodeo event." So I said, "Well, how do we do that?"

We get out the camera and our press passes, and there's a moment on the first day that I'm able to be down in the stadium — and I've never been down in the stadium on rodeo day, always in the stands. They start playing the national anthem, and you're down there with your photos and the photographers. They're playing the national anthem, and the F-15 jets fly over, and the pride of being an American is just bursting out of your chest, and you're in the rodeo and in a slightly dangerous place with your camera. You're going to tell this really cool story with the bucking broncos and the bull riders, and the stands are full. They're not here for me, but I'm going to get to tell people about this.

That was a point at which I said: This is really cool. There are a lot of fascinating things here that are fun to tell. There's something happening that we may never see again. I think that's probably the crux of it.

Don't you want to witness that thing you may never see again? We as newspaper reporters have an opportunity to be there.

HD video: http://www.whoneedsnewspapers.org/np_interviews.php?npld=epiphany &ivld=epiphany071

Richard Stein oversees the IT and graphics departments as well as Internet operations for The Garden Island's website. Before moving to Lihue, Stein began his newspaper career as the graphics/IT/website director for The East Oregonian in Pendleton, Ore. Stein began his printing career as a customer service representative for Century Publishing in Post Falls, Idaho. He is a graduate of the University of Idaho with a degree in fine arts and graphic design.

"Do's and Don'ts about Intrusiveness"

Korrie Wenzel, publisher
The Daily Republic
Mitchell, S.D.

In one of my first years in news, I covered a devastating tornado in Spencer, S.D., which is about 30 miles from here. It really showed me what it takes to be in this business, and the impact that you can have.

We competed directly. CNN and all these big networks brought satellite trucks, and the big newspapers were all here. Some of our competitors were there all the time, and the Associated Press brought in extra people, and here was The Daily Republic — this small town newspaper, 12,000 circulation — and I thought we held our own.

It taught me what it takes. But also it taught me, by watching how everyone else reacted in the media there, a lot of the do's and don'ts about intrusiveness and how you cover people. I learned that sometimes people just need to be left alone. I didn't feel that all the media outlets were very good about that during the Spencer tornado. That was a town of about 350 people.

When we got there early on, they were happy to visit with anybody, but as the days went on and the weeks wore on, they, understandably, became very tired of the media.

We like to think big, but we still have a heart and understand that these are our people here. The Spencer tornado probably more than anything put me in the direction of saying, "Newspapers can make a difference and people want to read you." They didn't have TV. Those people didn't have power. They didn't have anything, but they'd sure read The Daily Republic. Nothing made me prouder, and that was a great moment for us.

HD video: http://www.whoneedsnewspapers.org/np_interviews.php?npld=epiphany &ivld=epiphany098

Korrie Wenzel began his career at The Daily Republic as an 11-year-old carrier in his hometown of Wessington Springs, S.D. He joined the newsroom staff as a sports reporter in 1991 and later held various positions, including sports editor. assistant editor and editor. Wenzel was named publisher in 2010.

Section VII

AUTHORS' EPIPHANIES

Authors' Epiphanies

Sara Brown and Paul Steinle worked for many years in journalism — Sara Brown in newspapers and Paul Steinle in broadcast journalism and wire services. These are key moments in their careers when the power and purpose of journalism became evident to them.

"The Forefathers and Mothers Who Built Their Newspapers"

Sara Brown, Ph.D., secretary-treasurer
Valid Sources
Seattle, Wash.

In 1983, I moved from Vancouver, Wash., where I worked for The Columbian, a great midsized newspaper owned by the Campbell family, to Los Angeles to join another great family-owned newspaper—The Los Angeles Times, owned by the Chandler family.

The LA Times and the Times-Mirror corporate offices were located in one large city block in downtown L.A. The newspaper lobby was utilitarian, nothing fancy but a lot of hubbub with people coming and going.

I'd been at The Times for a couple of weeks when I was asked to meet a guest in the Times-Mirror corporate lobby. This was my first time on the other side of the block. By contrast, it was quiet. It felt like a museum with portraits of Times' leaders Harrison Gray Otis, Harry Chandler, Norman Chandler and Otis Chandler lining the walls. There were pictures, historic and current, of community dignitaries, political and business leaders and media moguls.

A number of the newspapers we visited for the "Who Needs Newspapers?" report were family owned. There were several we visited before we started to ask the question about epiphanies, beginning with the Mayo family at The Sequoyah County Times in Sallisaw, Okla.; the Hussman family at The Arkansas Democrat Gazette in Little Rock, Arkansas; the Gish family at The Mountain Eagle and the Shaw family at The Northwest Herald in Crystal Lake, Illinois. These papers also have their galleries of the forefathers and mothers who built their newspapers and played a significant role in the betterment of their communities.

I admit I was a small-town girl from Vancouver, Wash., that day in the Times-Mirror lobby, but I was inspired by the role The Times played in the development of Southern California. I continue to be proud of the locally owned newspapers that, through their sacrifice and commitment to their communities, bring history and continuity to the news they provide their readers and viewers.

Sara Brown, Ph.D., has more than 30 years experience as a human resource professional, management trainer, columnist and educator in the newspaper business. She was vice president of human resources at The Columbian (Vancouver, Wash.), and manager, organization development, at The Los Angeles Times. Brown is secretary-treasurer and cofounder of Valid Sources, a 501(c)(3). Brown has conducted leadership workshops for the ANPA (now NAA) written monthly columns for the NNA, and is a past president of the national NPRA. She has also advised small- and medium-sized newspapers, nationally, on human resource and organization issues. Brown holds an M.S., University of San Francisco, and a doctorate in human and organization systems, Fielding Graduate Institute.

"Showing Pictures about Major Problems on the News Could Change Things"

Paul Steinle, president
Valid Sources
Seattle, Wash.

In 1968, I was a young reporter working for WBZ-TV News in Boston. I had been working on a series of in-depth reports on the state's Youth Services Division, the state agency that both cared for and incarcerated troubled youth — so-called stubborn children and lawbreakers.

Since I was working in television, our challenge was to get inside a Youth Services building and film it. But the authorities were reluctant to grant us entry inside the locked-up buildings. One of the most notorious of the buildings was the benignly named Institute of Juvenile Guidance — housed in an archaic building within sight of the notorious Bridgewater State Mental Hospital, which had already been a cause *célèbre* because of Frederic Wiseman's first documentary, "The Titicut Follies."

Anyway, long story short — we learned that a member of the state's legislative oversight committee for Youth Services was going to visit the facility, so we tagged along with him and got our pictures inside on a winter day in 1969.

We found something that looked like a 19th century version of the Charles Addams Family mansion. It was gothic, outdated, and its heating system was broken — so half the building was boarded up. The place was horrible.

We showed the pictures on WBZ-TV in early 1969, just as a new governor, Frank Sargent, came into office. And, within a few weeks, Sargent dissolved the Youth Services Division and fired its director. We weren't the only news organization reporting on Youth Services, but the swiftness of the fallout shocked me. I also felt concern for the Youth Services director, whom I thought was an earnest man — though perhaps one who had not campaigned loudly enough to fix the system.

It was an aha moment. It taught me that showing pictures about major problems on the news could change things — and sometimes quickly. So you had better be sure you were fair and sure you were right — especially when someone's livelihood was at stake.

Paul Steinle is professor emeritus at Southern Oregon University, an adjunct professor at Quinnipiac University, and president and cofounder of Valid Sources, a 501(c)(3). Steinle is a veteran journalist and news media manager who has been teaching journalism since 1991. From 1991–2001, he launched graduate journalism programs at the University of Miami and Quinnipiac University; 2001–2010, he taught journalism and served as associate provost at Southern Oregon University, Ashland, Ore. Steinle served as president of the Sigma Delta Chi Foundation, 1995–2000. From 1961–1990, Steinle had a 29-year career as a professional reporter and news manager. He was the president of UPI and the Financial News Network; TV news director, KING-TV, Seattle; he reported from Saigon and Hong Kong for Group–W radio news, and he was a TV news producer and reporter at WBZ-TV and WCVB-TV in Boston, Mass. Steinle has an M.B.A., Harvard University, and an M.S., radio-TV, Syracuse University.

About Valid Sources

"To govern wisely, an authentic democracy needs an informed citizenry."
—Valid Sources

Whoneedsnewspapers.org is a project of Valid Sources, a 501 (c)(3). Valid Sources is a nonprofit organization formed to identify and promote excellent, ethically balanced journalism. Valid Sources' mission is to identify models of excellence that aspire "to seek the truth and report it," to document these activities and to raise these profiles. Valid Sources seeks to fulfill two key goals:

- Elevate public understanding of the value of professional, ethically balanced journalism, and
- Inform the journalism community of best journalism practices.

Valid Sources also aims to inform the public and the new disseminators of news about the value of media sources that strive to "seek truth and report it." This goal reflects the language that frames the ethical code of the Society of Professional Journalists (http://www.spj.org/ethicscode. asp): "Seek truth and report it." This lofty aspiration is the foundation of a journalistic ethic that drives journalism education and is reflected in the code of ethics of many major news organizations. Valid Sources seeks to reinforce this mission by identifying those news organizations and individuals who aspire to this goal, explaining how those news organizations do it, why they do it, and how the communities they serve benefit from these best journalism practices. To further this mission, Valid Sources created the www.WhoNeedsNewspapers.org website. Please see the site for details. For more information about Valid Sources contact: Paul Steinle or Sara Brown at: Valid Sources, 1916 Pike Place, Ste. 12, Seattle, Wash. 98101; (541) 941-8116; paul (or sara)@whoneedsnewspapers.org.

Index